Swing Trade Strategies

The complete beginners guide to make money with stocks using swing trading strategies for short term investing, day trading and option trading

By

Simon Jordan

© **Copyright 2020 by (Simon Jordan) - All rights reserved.**

This document is geared towards providing exact and reliable information in regards to the topic and issue covered. The publication is sold with the idea that the publisher is not required to render accounting, officially permitted, or otherwise, qualified services. If advice is necessary, legal or professional, a practiced individual in the profession should be ordered.

- From a Declaration of Principles which was accepted and approved equally by a Committee of the American Bar Association and a Committee of Publishers and Associations.

In no way is it legal to reproduce, duplicate, or transmit any part of this document in either electronic means or in printed format. Recording of this publication is strictly prohibited and any storage of this document is not allowed unless with written permission from the publisher. All rights reserved.

The information provided herein is stated to be truthful and consistent, in that any liability, in terms of inattention or otherwise, by any usage or abuse of any policies, processes, or directions contained within is the solitary and utter responsibility of the recipient reader. Under no circumstances will any legal responsibility or blame be held against the publisher for any reparation, damages, or monetary loss due to the information herein, either directly or indirectly.

Respective authors own all copyrights not held by the publisher.

The information herein is offered for informational purposes solely, and is universal as so. The presentation of the information is without contract or any type of guarantee assurance.

The trademarks that are used are without any consent, and the publication of the trademark is without permission or backing by the trademark owner. All trademarks and brands within this book are for clarifying purposes only and are owned by the owners themselves, not affiliated with this document.

Table of Content

INTRODUCTION 6

CHAPTER 1: UNDERSTANDING SWING TRADING 10

1.1 Swing Trading vs Day Trading 12

1.2 Swing Trading Vs Position Trading 18

1.3 Different Market Participants (Retail vs Institutional Traders) 22

1.4 How to Start Trading? 26

1.5 Buying Long or Selling Short 29

CHAPTER 2: TOOLS AND PLATFORMS FOR SWING TRADING 32

2.1 Platforms for Swing Trading 32

2.2 Tools Available Online 34

2.3 Financial Instruments for Swing Trading 38

2.4 Assessing the Risk and the Reward 48

CHAPTER 3: FUNDAMENTAL TECHNICAL ANALYSIS .52

3.1 Fundamental Analysis Factors 53

3.2 Support and Resistance Levels 57

3.3 Moving Averages 64

3.4 Relative Strength Index 70

3.5 MACD: Convergence and Divergence 74

3.6 Technical Analysis – Patterns 78

CHAPTER 4: SWING TRADING GUIDING PRINCIPLES 85

4.1 Defining and Building Routine Strategies 86

4.2 Option trading advanced technique for Swing Trading 90

CONCLUSION 97

Introduction

Swing trading is portrayed as a sort of essential trading in which positions are held for longer than a single day. Most fundamentalists are swing brokers since changes in corporate basics by and large require a few days or even seven days to make adequate value development render a sensible benefit.

In any case, this depiction of swing trading is a disentanglement. As a general rule, swing trading sits in the continuum between day trading to slant trading. An informal investor will hold a stock anyplace from a couple of moments to a couple of hours yet never over a day; a pattern broker looks at the drawn-out central patterns of a stock or record and may hold the stock for half a month or months. Swing traders hold a specific stock for a while, by and large, a couple of days to a little while, which is between those boundaries, and they will exchange the stock based on its intra-week or intra-month motions among good faith and negativity.

Most fundamentalists are swing brokers since changes in corporate essentials by and large require a few days or even seven days to make adequate value development render a sensible benefit. Swing trading is outstanding amongst other trading styles for the starting dealer to get their feet wet, yet it despite everything offers noteworthy benefit potential for transitional and propelled brokers. Swing dealers get fair criticism on their exchanges following two or three days to keep them inspired, however, their long and short places of a few days are of the length that doesn't prompt interruption. On the other hand, pattern trading offers more prominent benefit potential if a dealer can get a significant market pattern of weeks or months, however, few are the traders with adequate order to hold a place that long without getting diverted. Then again, trading many stocks every day may demonstrate too white-knuckle of a ride for a few, making swing trading the ideal medium between the limits.

Swing trading sits in the continuum between day trading to drift trading. The primary key to effective swing trading is picking the right stocks. The best applicants are large cap stocks, which are among the most effectively exchanged stocks on the significant trades. In a functioning business sector, these stocks will swing between extensively characterized high and low limits, and the swing dealer will ride the wave one way for two or three days or weeks to change to the contrary side of the exchange when the stock turns around its directions.

In both of the two market boundaries, the bear market advertises condition or seething buyer showcase market, swing trading seems to end up being a preferably extraordinary test over in a market between these two limits. In these boundaries, even the most dynamic stocks won't display the equivalent here and their motions as when records are generally steady for half a month or months. In a bear market or buyer showcase, energy will, by and large, convey stocks for an extensive period one way just, in this way affirming the best procedure is to exchange based on the more extended term directional pattern.

The swing trader, in this manner, is best situated when markets are going no place – when files ascend for a few days, at that point decrease for the following hardly any days, to rehash a similar general example and once more. A few months may go with significant stocks and lists generally at the same spot as their different levels, yet the swing broker has numerous chances to get the transient developments here and there (now and then inside a channel).

The issue with both swing trading and long haul pattern transferring is that achievement depends on accurately distinguishing what kind of market is right now being experienced. Pattern trading would have been the perfect system for the positively trending business sector of the last 50% of the 1990s, while swing trading presumably would have been best for 2000 and 2001.

Basic moving midpoints (SMAs) offer help and obstruction levels, just as bullish and bearish examples. Backing and opposition levels can flag whether to purchase a stock. Bullish and bearish hybrid examples signal value focuses where you ought to enter and leave shares.

The exponential moving standard (EMA) is a variety of the SMA that places more emphasis on the most recent information focuses. The EMA gives brokers clear pattern signs and passage and leaves quicker than a straightforward moving normal. The EMA hybrid can be utilized in swing trading to time passage and leave focuses.

An essential EMA hybrid framework can be utilized by concentrating on the nine-, 13-and 50-period EMAs. A bullish hybrid happens when the value crosses over these moving midpoints in the wake of being underneath. This implies an inversion might be likely to work out and that an upswing might be starting. At the point when the nine-time frame EMA crosses over the 13-time frame EMA, it flags a long section. In any case, the 13-time frame EMA must be over the 50-time frame EMA or cross above it.

Then again, a bearish hybrid happens when the cost of security falls underneath these EMAs. This signals a possible inversion of a pattern, and it very well may be utilized to time an exit of a long position. At the point when the nine-time frame EMA crosses beneath the 13-time frame EMA, it flags a short section or a door of a long post. Be that as it may, the 13-time frame EMA needs to be beneath the 50-time frame EMA or cross underneath it.

Much exploration on chronicled information has demonstrated that, in a market helpful for swing trading, liquid stocks will in the general exchange above and under a standard worth, which is depicted on a diagram with an EM). In this book, "Come into My Trading Room: A Complete Guide of Trading" (2002), Dr Alexander Elder uses his comprehension of a stock's conduct above and beneath the standard to portray the swing broker's technique of "purchasing commonality and selling madness" or "shorting regularity and covering despondency." Once the swing merchant has utilized the EMA to recognize the run of the mill gauge on the stock outline, the individual goes long at the pattern when the stock is going up and short at the benchmark when the stock is on its way down.

In this way, swing dealers are not hoping to hit the grand slam with a solitary exchange – they are not worried about the ideal chance to purchase a stock precisely at its base and sell precisely at its top (or the other way around). In a perfect trading condition, they trust that the stock will hit its gauge and affirm its heading before they make their moves. The story gets increasingly convoluted when a more grounded upturn or downturn is affecting everything: the broker may incomprehensibly go long when the stock plunges beneath its EMA and trust that the stock will return up in an upswing, or the person in question may short a stock that has wounded over the EMA and hang tight for it to drop if the more drawn out pattern is down.

At the point when it comes time to take benefits, the swing merchant will need to leave the exchange as close as conceivable to the upper or lower channel line without being excessively exact, which may cause the danger of passing up on the best chance. In a substantial market, when a stock is showing a solid directional pattern, dealers can hang tight for the channel line to be reached before taking their benefit. Yet, in a more vulnerable market, they may make their interests before the line is hit (if the heading changes and the front doesn't get caught on that specific swing).

Chapter 1: Understanding Swing Trading

Swing trading includes holding a position either long or short for more than one transferring meeting, yet ordinarily not longer than a little while or two or three months. This is a general period, as individual exchanges may last longer than two or three months, yet the dealer may even now think of them as swing exchanges. Swing exchanges can likewise happen during a trading meeting.

The objective of swing trading is to catch a lump of a potential value move. While a few brokers search out unpredictable stocks with loads of development, others may favor progressively calm shares. In either case, swing trading is the way toward distinguishing where an advantage's cost is probably going to move straight away, entering a position, and afterwards catching a lump of the benefit if that move appears.

Fruitful swing traders are just hoping to catch a lump of the average value move and afterwards proceed onward to the following chance.

Swing trading is one of the most well-known types of dynamic trading, where traders search for the middle of the road term openings utilizing different kinds of specialized investigation. In case you're keen on swing trading, you ought to be personally acquainted with the specialized examination.

Many swing dealer's survey exchanges on a hazard/reward premise. By dissecting the diagram of an advantage, they figure out where they will enter, where they will put a stop misfortune, and afterwards foresee where they can get out with a benefit. If they are gambling $1 per share on an arrangement that could sensibly deliver a $3 gain that is an ideal hazard/reward. Then again, betting $1 to make $1 or just make $0.75 isn't exactly as positive.

Swing brokers fundamentally utilize specialized investigation because of the momentary idea of the exchanges. The critical examination can be used to upgrade the research. For instance, if a swing merchant sees a bullish arrangement in stock, they might need to check that the basics of the benefit look positive or are improving moreover.

Swing brokers will frequently search for circumstances on the day by day graphs and may watch 1-hour or 15-minute diagrams to discover exact passage, stop misfortune, and take benefit levels.

A swing dealer will in general search for multi-day graph designs. A portion of the more typical examples includes moving standard hybrids, cup-and-handle models, head and shoulders patterns, banners, and triangles. Essential inversion candles might be utilized, notwithstanding different markers to devise a robust trading plan.

At last, each swing dealer devises an arrangement and methodology that gives them an edge over numerous exchanges. This includes searching for exchange arrangements that will, in general lead to unsurprising developments in the benefit's cost. This isn't simple, and no technique or method works without fail. With a positive reward, winning each time isn't required. The more positive the hazard/prize of a trading system, the fewer occasions it needs to win to create a comprehensive benefit over numerous exchanges.

Real-World Example of Swing Trade in Apple

AAPL's stock price from May 2018 through December 2018 exhibiting several technical patterns potentially suitable for swing trading.

A real-world example of possible AAPL swing trading chances.

This was accompanied by a small cup and handle design, which often signals a continuance of the price getting higher so if the stock moves above the high rise of the handle.

In this case:

The cost ascends over the handle, setting off a potential purchase close $192.70.

One potential spot to put a stop to misfortune is underneath the handle, set apart by the square shape, close to $187.50.

In light of the section and stop-misfortune, the assessed hazard for the exchange is $5.20 per share ($192.70 - $187.50).

In the event that searching for a potential prize that is at any rate double the hazard, any cost above $203.10 ($192.70 + (2 *$5.20)) will give this.

Beside a hazard/reward, the merchant could likewise use other leave strategies, for example, trusting that the cost will make an extraordinary failure. With this technique, a leave signal wasn't given until $216.46, when the cost dipped under the earlier pullback low. This technique would have brought about a benefit of $23.76 per share. Thought of another way - a 12% benefit in return for under 3% hazard. This swing exchange took around two months.

Other leave procedures could be utilized when the value crosses under a moving normal (not appeared), or when a marker, for example, the stochastic oscillator crosses its sign line.

1.1 Swing Trading vs Day Trading

The period on which a dealer selects to exchange can significantly affect transferring technique and gainfulness. Informal investors open and close various situations inside a single day, while swing brokers take exchanges that last many days, weeks or even months. These two distinctive trading styles can suit different traders relying upon the measure of capital accessible, time accessibility, brain research, and the market being traded.

One trading style isn't better than another, and it truly comes down to which style suits a broker's very own conditions. A few traders pick to do either, while others might be informal investors, swing dealers and purchase-and-hold financial specialists at the same time.

Likely Returns

Day trading pulls in dealers searching for quick exacerbating of profits. Expect a vendor to risk 0.5% of their capital on each trade. In case they lose, they'll Miss 0.5%, anyway in case they win they'll make 1% (2:1 prize to-danger extent).

Moreover, acknowledge they win half of their trades. They will add about 1.5% to their record balance each day, less trading costs. They are making even 1% a day would grow a trading account by over 200% through the range of the year, uncompounded.

On the opposite side, while the numbers seem, by all accounts, to be anything besides hard to recreate for tremendous returns, nothing's ever that straightforward. Making twice as much on victors as you lost on disappointments, while moreover winning a portion of the significant number of trades you take, doesn't come with no issue. You can make rapid augmentations; nonetheless, you can likewise rapidly deplete your trading account through day trading.

Swing trading aggregates increases and misfortunes more gradually than day trading; however, you can, in any case, have individual swing exchanges that rapidly bring about significant gains or troubles. Accept a swing dealer utilizes a similar hazard the board rule and dangers 0.5% of their capital

14

on each exchange to attempt to make 1% to 2% on their triumphant exchanges.

Accept they gain 1.5% on average for winning exchanges, losing 0.5% on losing trades. They do six trades for each month and win half of those trades. In a race of the mill month, the swing broker could earn 3% for the balance, fewer charges through the span of the year, that comes out to about 36%, which sounds excellent yet offers less potential than an informal investor's conceivable income.

These model situations serve to represent the qualification between the two trading styles. Changing the level of exchanges won, the average win contrasted with ordinary misfortune, or the number of transactions, will influence a procedure's earning potential.

When in doubt, day trading has more benefit potential, at any rate on littler records. As the size of history develops, it gets increasingly hard to use all the capital on transient day exchanges viably.

Informal investors may discover their rate returns decrease the more capital they have. Their dollar returns can even now go up, since making 5% on $1 million compares to considerably more than 20% on $100,000. Swing traders have less possibility of this event.

Shifting Capital Requirements

Capital necessities differ as per the market being trading. Day trading and swing brokers can begin with varying measures of capital relying upon whether they trade the stock, forex, or prospects advertise.

Day trading stocks the US requires a record equalization of at any rate $25,000. No lawful least exists to swing exchange stocks, albeit a swing broker will probably need to have in any event $10,000 in their record, and ideally $20,000 if hoping to draw a salary from trading.

Today exchange the forex advertisement, no legitimate least exists; however, it is suggested that traders start within any event $500, yet ideally $1,000 or more. To swing exchange forex, the base recommended is about $1,500, however ideally more. This measure of capital will permit you to enter in any event a couple of exchanges one after another.

Today exchange prospects start within any event $5,000 to $7,500, and increasing capital would be stunningly better. These sums rely upon the fates contract being exchanged. Day trading a few agreements could require considerably more capital, while a couple of deals, for example, miniaturized scale contracts, may require less.

To swing exchange an assortment of fates contracts, you need at any rate $10,000, and likely $20,000 or more. The sum required relies upon the edge prerequisites of the particular agreement being exchanged.

Trading Times Differ

Both days trading and swing trading require time. Yet, day trading usually occupies substantially more time—informal investors as a rule exchange for at any rate two hours out of each day. Including planning time and outline/trading survey implies spending, in any event, three to four hours at the PC, at the very least. On the off chance that an informal investor selects to exchange for more than several hours every day, the time speculation goes up significantly, and it turns into an all-day work.

Swing trading, then again, can take substantially less time. For instance, in case you're swing trading off an everyday graph, you could discover new exchanges and update orders on current situations in around 45 minutes per night. These exercises may not be required on a daily premise.

Some swing dealers, taking exchanges that last weeks or months, may just need to search for transactions and update arrays once every week, bringing the time responsibility down to about an hour of the week rather than every night, or refreshing requests may not be required on a daily premise.

You should likewise do day trading while a market is open and dynamic. The best hours for day trading are constrained to specific times of the day. If you can't day exchange during those hours, at that point pick swing trading as a superior choice. Swing dealers can search for transactions or spot orders whenever of day, much after the market has shut.

Swing dealers are less influenced constantly to-second changes in the cost of a benefit. They center on the master plan, commonly seeing common diagrams, so setting exchanges after the market closes on a specific day works fine and dandy. Informal investors bring in cash off second-by-second developments, so they should be included while the activity is occurring.

Center, Time, and Practice

Swing trading and day trading both require a decent arrangement of work and information to create benefits reliably, although the information requested isn't really "book smarts." Fruitful trading comes about because of finding a system that delivers an edge, or a benefit over countless exchanges, and afterwards executing that methodology again and again.

Some information available being exchanged and one gainful technique can begin creating pay, alongside parts and heaps of training. Everyday costs move uniquely in contrast to they did in the past, which implies the dealer should have the option to execute their system under different conditions and adjust as conditions change. This presents a troublesome test. Reliable outcomes just originate from rehearsing a system under heaps of various market situations. That requires some serious energy and ought to include making many exchanges a demo account before gambling natural capital.

Picking day trading or swing trading likewise comes down to character. Day trading ordinarily includes more pressure, requires supported concentration for broadened timeframes and takes unimaginable control. Individuals that like activity, have quick reflexes, and additionally like computer games and poker will in general incline toward day trading.

Swing trading occurs at a slower pace, with any longer passes between activities like entering or leaving exchanges. It can even now be high pressure and requires excellent control and persistence.

It doesn't require as much supported center, so if you experience, issues remaining centered, swing trading might be the better alternative. Quick reflexes don't make a difference in swing swapping as exchanges can be taken after the market closes and costs have entirely moved.

Day trading and swing trading both offer opportunity for the feeling that a broker works for themselves. Dealers ordinarily chip away at their own, and they are answerable for financing their records and for all misfortunes and benefits produced. One can contend that swing brokers have more opportunity as far as time since swing trading occupies less time than day trading.

A Final Comparison

One trading style isn't better than the other; they simply suit contrasting requirements. Day trading has more benefit potential, in any event in rate terms on littler measured transferring accounts. Swing dealers have a superior possibility of keeping up their rate returns even as their record develops, in a specific way.

Capital prerequisites change a considerable amount over the various markets and trading styles. Day trading requires additional time than swing trading, while both take a lot of training to pick up consistency. Day trading makes an ideal choice for the activity sweethearts. Those looking for a lower-stress and less time-serious alternative can grasp swing trading.

The balance doesn't give venture, duty or monetary counsel and administrations. The data is applied without consideration of a specific financial specialist's venture goals, hazard resistance or money-related circumstances and therefore won't be fair for all investors. Previous execution is not indicative of future performance. Contributing involves chance along with the possible head loss.

1.2 Swing Trading Vs Position Trading

Position Trading is otherwise called "purchase and hold." It is a typical methodology among value speculators who regularly allude to it as Trend Trading as it can include comparative techniques for pattern distinguishing proof before building up a position. In any case, in the spread wagering and CFD universes, it can allude to a place which is either purchased or offered to open. Most definitely, it varies from Trend Trading basically in that exchanges are typically held for longer time frames – frequently numerous months.

Be that as it may, for both value brokers and spread betters, Position Trading places a more prominent accentuation on essential investigation than would be done in Trend Trading. If considering an individual stock, this will include acquiring a decent understanding of what the organization does, where it works and the potential for development or development. It will likewise involve contemplating the organization's budget reports with specific accentuation on the financial record and benefit and misfortune account. Position traders will need to guarantee that the organization is monetarily secure and isn't stacked up on obligation – in any event when contrasted with rivals inside a similar division. They will need to guarantee that the organization's stock isn't overrated against different stocks in the same division and the more extensive market all in all. Ordinarily, speculators will take a gander at the cost per share/income per share (P/E) proportion to check whether the organization is genuinely esteemed. The Position Trader will endeavor to guarantee that a specific organization has a decent item stream, or offers a new item with high boundaries to passage for contenders. Likewise, it is very much run and monetarily stable. It is at precisely that point that the Position Trader takes a gander at outlines and specialized markers to set up section, exit and stops levels for the exchange. If any of these don't make any sense, at that point, the Position Trader will hold off and hang tight for better-trading chances somewhere else.

Position Traders tend not to stress over transient variances and instead attempt to benefit from the more drawn out term patterns. This has the bit of leeway that once the exchange is entered, it doesn't require steady observing. It sounds simple; however, Position Trading isn't for everybody. A Position Trader must show restraint enough to kick back and trust that an exchange will play out. They should have the order to adapt to a place that betrays them (for the time being) remembering the purposes behind entering the exchange in the first spot. In any case, the Position Trader should likewise be prepared to recognize when a transaction has turned out badly, regularly when there is an adjustment in the basics fundamental, the first choice to take the position. Likewise, with all trading, cautious hazard and cash man

Expectations and Trading Style Preferences

For some financial specialists, an opportunity to receive a particular trading style is made with their short-and long haul objectives at the top of the priority list. For instance, if a broker is foreseeing unstable value activity in a given resource throughout the following week, they are bound to embrace a temporary situation in the stock as opposed to a long haul.

Speculators who are looking to build up feasible "savings" for their retirement years will, in all probability, investigate different position trading choices instead of swing trading. This is expected in massive part to the way that these people in all likelihood have the advantage of time on their side and don't have to take on the hazard required to open the entryway for fast, momentary benefits.

For those people who are excited about getting by as an expert trader, swing trading and day trading are undeniably more practical alternatives than position trading. This is because of the way that most position trading includes not many genuine exchanges being made, while swing trading and day trading expect financial specialists to play an unmistakably increasingly dynamic job all the while.

Recognizing Market Climate

Before you start an exchange, you ought to be exceptionally mindful of which explicit trading system you plan on utilizing with that specific resource. For instance, on the off possibility that you have chosen to buy 100 portions of stock "X," you should as of now have a genuinely smart thought with regards to whether you will hold the stock for quite a long time, days, months or years. Although it is entirely sensible to adjust your perspective concerning your technique after some time, intentionally abstaining from considering your alternatives will improve the probability that you will lose cash over the long run instead of benefit from your venture.

For some financial specialists, the main thought when deciding to buy a stock ought to be whether the market all in all is showing bullish or bearish patterns. On the off chance that the market has entered an out and out "bull run," you ought to gauge your alternatives cautiously before entering a drawn-out position. This is because of the way that the market will probably encounter an adjustment sooner or later after the finish of the bullish pattern. This revision could break down the benefits you made when you bought your stock, especially if the value point where you procured the advantage was well over its right valuation.

On the furthest edge of the range, a drawn-out bearish pattern in the commercial center may flag a perfect chance to enter a drawn-out situation on a stock. The choice to open a position following a bearish pattern will fundamentally be founded on whether or not the trader accepts the bear advert has finished, and further misfortunes won't follow. Choices, for example, will significantly affect the potential benefit anticipating a trader, as the inability to pursue accessible investigation properly accurately could make noteworthy misfortunes. As usual, it is essential that traders complete; however, much exploration and examination could reasonably be expected to decide if a specific exchange coordinates their venture objectives.

Pushing Ahead with Your Trades

On the off chance that you have been asking yourself, "Which is the best venture for long haul trading?" The disappointing truth is that there essentially is no "right" response to this inquiry. Given the general flightiness of the commercial center, there is consistently a component of hazard engaged with all exchanges, paying little heed to the amount of a "definite wager" they may at first appear.

In light of that, it is strongly suggested that beginner traders abstain from receiving any trading positions without first counselling any of the wide-going instructive assets on the web or enrolling the administrations of a venture guide. A large number of online businesses working today give counselling administrations to dealers.

This information stage might be necessary for recently stamped financial specialists looking to set themselves up in the present unique commercial center. Notwithstanding which systems are utilized, it is consistently essential to recollect not to contribute a more significant number of assets than you can stand to lose, as all adding convey some level of risk management is indispensable.

1.3 Different Market Participants (Retail vs Institutional Traders)

Presently after talking about the distinctive trading styles that can be utilized in the business sectors, we should take a gander at the various kinds of traders who are using these swapping styles. Retail traders are free individuals who are likely transferring from a home office. Retail traders can be low maintenance dealers or full-time brokers, yet they are not working for a firm, and they are not overseeing others' cash. Even though it is a lot higher than contrasted with even five years prior, Retail dealers despite everything make up a generally little level of the all-out day by day trading volume of the market.

An ever-increasing number of individuals are striking out all alone and doing their own self-coordinated contribution. The internet, with its plenty of data and devices, has determined this pattern, alongside the chance to exchange online without the utilization of an expert representative. Numerous financial specialists have found that with a little work they can match or better the presentation of a large number of the joint store directors, particularly when considering the now and again extravagant administration expenses being charged by these cash chiefs.

The more prominent classification of dealers in the market is the Institutional brokers, which incorporate the Wall Street venture banks, private trading firms (called prop traders), common assets and speculative stock investments. A great deal of their trading depends on muddled PC programs (additionally called calculations). Much of the time, there are no people legitimately engaged with the trading activities of these enormous records? These Institutional brokers have impressive cash behind them, and they are advanced. These folks are professionals and, as a Retail broker, you have to remember that. These are the individuals and machines that you are going up against. Retail dealers can rival them; however, you need the proper devices and an all-around considered arrangement.

Singular Retail dealers do have a few points of interest over Institutional brokers. These Institutional brokers are roused to exchange regularly and in huge volumes. In correlation, Retail traders can sit tight for a decent arrangement and exchange whenever they see a suitable hazard to remunerate opportunity. Institutional traders likewise have massive records and can't move their cash all through a situation as promptly as a Retail dealer. An Institutional broker won't take a 1,000 offer situation in the supply of a little organization that exchanges 250,000 offers per day. It is merely excessively small for them to trouble.

Joint assets and comparable Institutional traders may likewise have inherent reserve limitations that keep them from purchasing stocks that exchange under a specific cost or have a market capitalization under a particular level (advertise capitalization is the all-out estimation of the entirety of the portions of an organization, for instance, if an organization has 1,000,000 offers, and they are trading at $10.00 every, at that point their market capitalization is $10,000,000.00). This leaves some open stock doors for the Retail trader that bigger establishments can't take an interest in.

Amusingly, enormous quantities of individual Retail brokers won't utilize this preferred position to their advantage, and for different reasons, they will rather overtrade. They capitulate to covetousness and dread, and that makes them exchange rashly. Rather than being patient and practicing the self-control of champs, they become washouts by overtrading. Retail traders who need to be successful in Trading with the experts must show restraint. They should likewise perceive and deal with the brain science of dread and greed and how it influences a dealer's activities.

With swing trading, you are hanging tight for a chance to move all through the market in a generally brief timeframe to produce benefits while downplaying your hazard. That timeframe can be as short as for the time being (from the market close on one day to the opening of the market on the accompanying trading day) to up to a little while or more. You would prefer fundamentally not to outfox or beat these Institutional traders. Actually, you might be trading with them and taking similar places that they are building or previously holding. It never hurts to hitch a ride on their journey transport. However, your bit of leeway is that you can bounce on and off of the boat rapidly, while it takes them significantly longer to stop or alter course. As a Retail dealer, you are hanging tight for a chance to arrive at your benefit target and either sell or begin to scale out of your position.

Dealing with your hazard is additionally more straightforward as a Retail trader. You can follow your trading plan and leave your losing positions rapidly if the stock you are holding doesn't move as you anticipated. This is substantially more troublesome if a trader is holding a few hundred thousand offers or more in an Institutional record.

As a Retail trader, you can likewise play stocks that other Retail financial specialists are performing. Monitoring online networking locales like Stock Twits and Twitter will give you a decent feeling of where Retail financial specialists are putting away their cash, be that as it may, don't become involved with the points of interest of the entirety of the posts. There are loads of jokes on Stock Twits making wild expectations and touting how they simply made $7,000.00 on an exchange XYZ Company. Take all that you read with a massive grain of salt.

A Retail dealer can utilize these web-based life locales for their potential benefit in a few different ways. To start with, utilize these destinations to discover where different dealers are playing. You can use the play area similarity – on the off chance that you are in a play area at the most distant corner of the field and a lot of individuals are playing soccer on the opposite side of the field; you're not in the game. Hot stocks and areas will appear as drifting in web-based social networking - a swing dealer ought to consistently be taking the path of least resistance, particularly on the off chance that they're playing energy type exchanges.

Another approach to utilize internet based life is to follow a bunch of trustworthy traders and banners. These dealers make significant posts like, "MU is ricocheting off the 50-day moving normal and may go higher," versus an insignificant job like, "I simply made $6,000.00 purchasing and selling Micron." There is an immense bit of leeway to being in a network of keen brokers for reaping thoughts and getting other "astute" suppositions and considerations on singular stocks and the market.

Summing up, as a swing trader, you should be cautious that you are not on an inappropriate side of the exchange against either Institutional or other Retail dealers. Institutional traders can move markets. However, they attempt to purchase in or sell out of positions without contorting costs through forceful purchasing or selling. As a Retail financial specialist, you will never know without a doubt what these foundations are doing, so you have to depend on the outlines and your specialized investigation to assist you with perusing the market feeling. You can frequently observe where Retail speculators are playing by watching online life and utilizing different specialized instruments.

1.4 How to Start Trading?

Possibly there's an item you utilize so much that companions or family members state you should purchase stock in the organization. Or then again maybe you got a bonus and need to put a bit of it in the market for no particular reason and, if all works out in the right way, benefit.

In case you're tingling to get hands-on some dynamic web-based trading, this guide will help kick you off.

1. Choose if this is the correct methodology for

Suppose you've maximized 401(k) synchronize dollars from your boss, and you've additionally begun putting resources into an IRA. Generally, 401(k) plans don't permit members to buy singular stocks - instead, financial specialists look over a determination of shared and record reserves. Yet, you can ordinarily purchase and exchange commodities inside an IRA account. Trading inside an IRA can be helpful: Because these records are advantaged, charges on capital increases will be conceded or stayed away from totally.

You've contributed the yearly maximal to a 401(k) and an IRA and are likely on target to meet retirement objectives. You're likewise willing and ready to take on more hazard by stock exchanges. For this situation, you should open an available investment fund with an online dealer and trade inside that account.

Trading singular stock not just conveys more hazard, it requires more exertion than putting resources into universal or file reserves. You have to effectively watch your positions and get whether and how to respond to showcase moves.

(Peruse increasingly about the rudiments of purchasing stocks here.) This isn't the sort of risk is most retirement financial specialists need to take on.

2. Get instruction

Before you trade anything, get the hang of all that you can about contributing and the business sectors. Slip-ups can be expensive.

There is a great deal of free instructive assets that instruct how to exchange through an online specialist. Think about Morningstar's Investing Classroom or one of the contributing seminars on Udemy.com.

Likewise, most stock traders offer their instructive focuses and staff of previous brokers or speculation counsellors who can control you. A few intermediaries, for example, TD Ameritrade, offer their customers paper trading, a reenactment of transferring that is an extraordinary method to rehearse without cash or hazard included.

3. Select an online trader

Pick an online trader with the devices and backing to coordinate your needs. On the off possibility that you as of now know what you need, you can think about your alternatives while examining the best traders:

As a rule, novice dealers ought to organize client care, instructive assets, and record and exchange essentials. Furthermore, consider the online specialist's stock trading programming. New brokers will need a stage that is smoothed out, simple to explore and joins how-to exhortation and a trader network of companions to help answer questions.

4. Begin exploring stocks

Your record is opened, and you're prepared to start contributing. What's straightaway? Picking stocks, obviously, and that is the bristly part.

Most brokers start by doing an exhaustive examination of an organization, taking a gander at open data including income reports, financial filings and SEC reports, just as outside exploration reports from proficient investigators. Quite a lot of this ought to be given by your trader, alongside ongoing organization news and hazard appraisals.

Start gradually, picking a couple of stocks and contributing a set measure of cash that you are set up to lose. You can furrow restores into the capital — or different organizations — yet don't add more money to the pot until you recognize what you're doing and can place examinations into various organizations.

5. Make an arrangement and stick to it so

Contribution can be passionate, especially for those new to the game. Losing money doesn't feel better, and it's anything but difficult to frenzy and pull out at an inappropriate period. It's extra simple to get cleared up in the energy of what feels like a triumphant stock.

That is the reason it's essential to arrange for the amount you need to give at what price and decide how far you're willing to let a stock fall before you get out. Utilizing the correct sort of exchange demand can assist you with remaining on design and keep away from passionate reactions. For instance, stop-misfortune orders trigger a deal if a stock drops to a specific value, which can limit hazard and misfortunes.

1.5 Buying Long or Selling Short

With respect to securities exchange trading, the long and short terms refer to whether a transaction is triggered by first purchase or first sale.

- Large transactions are begun by purchasing with the intention to sell later at a more significant price and knowing the value.
- A fast sale is facilitated by selling stocks at a lower cost and knowing the benefit before buying.

Long term Trades

At the time when an informal investor is in a lengthy exchange, they have bought a benefit and are holding on to sell when the cost goes up. Day dealers regularly will utilize the expressions "purchase" and "long" conversely.

In fact, some trading programming has a "purchase" verified exchange section button, whereas others have "long" marked exchange section captures. The phrase is commonly used to represent a vacant condition, as in "1 am long Apple," which indicates that the broker already owns parts of Apple Inc.

Long Trade Potential

Vendors regularly state that they are "going fast" or "going long" to show their eagerness to purchase a particular commodity. If you go long at $10,000 on 1,000 segments of XYZ stock, the trade will cost you $10,000. You'll get $10,200, and net a $200 profit, less fees, on the off chance you can sell the proposals at $10.20. This is the ideal outcome when you go far.

Exactly when you go far, the opportunity for profit is infinite, as the cost of the advantageous position will increase confusion. When you buy 100 parts of stock at $1, the price could go up to $2, $5, $50, $100, etc., given the fact the casual speculators are usually trading for even more diminutive moves.

The other side is a decrease to enable an increase of costs. In the off chance of selling your bids at $9.90, you'll get $9.900 back in your $10,000 bill. You lose $100, with transaction costs added.

The greatest potential misfortune in this design is if the value of the bid drops to $0, which results in a $1 mistake for every deal. Informal investors also strive to keep risks and rewards under close track, seeking frequent rewards from various small steps to keep away from massive drops in value.

Short Trades

Shorting a stock is frustrating for most new traders as we normally have to buy something to sell it in practice. Informal buyers are selling capital in short markets until they get them and are optimistic the cost will go down. They understand a benefit if the value they rely on is greater than the price at which they sell. You can purchase and then sell, or sell, and then purchase in the monetary markets.

Informal investors use the terms "sell" and "buy" on a daily basis vice versa. Correspondingly, some trading programming has an exchange segment button stamped "sell," whereas some have an exchange transfer button checked "short." The word short is commonly used to represent an empty condition, as in "I am short SPY," which shows the shipper has a short situation in the S&P 500 (SPY) ETF at present. Vendors typically say that I'm "going short" or "going short" to demonstrate their eagerness to shortcut a specific commodity (to sell what they don't have).

Short Trade Potential

In case you go quick on 1,000 segments of XYZ stock at $10, like the instance of going big, you get $10,000 into your ledger. It is not your money anyway, in any event. The record will prove you have-1,000 offers and you can restore the balance to zero by buying 1,000 offers at some stage or another. You have no idea what the benefit or disadvantage of your position is, unless you do it accordingly.

Unless you can buy the offers at $9.60, you'll pay $9,600 for the 1,000 offers. You got $10,000 at first when you first went short and your benefit is $400, less commissions. You pay $10,200 for those 1,000 deals, and you lose $200, given bonuses, on the off chance that the stock is worth ascents and you repurchase the proposals at $10.20.

Your benefit is compelled to combine you from the start jumped onto the system exactly when you go short. Your risk, however, is limitless as the cost could rise to $10, $50, or more. The latter case means you'd have to pay $5,000 to buy back the sales, losing $4,500. Given that informal investors work to track hazards on all exchanges, this situation is typically not a problem for casual investors (ideally) taking short positions.

Shorting or undercutting helps expert dealers to profit from whether or not the market is rising or declining, which is the reason why professional traders generally assume that the market is going, not the way it is running.

Shorting Various Markets

Investors in most budgetary markets can be going down. A dealer will constantly go low on the fates and forex markets. Some stocks are also short-capable (ready to be sold and then purchased) in the sale of shares, though not all of them.

To be concise on the financial exchange, your agent will get the offers from someone who owns the plans, and if the specialist can't get the ideas for you, he won't let you shorten the stock. Furthermore, stocks that have just started trading on the trade — called Initial Public Offering Stocks (IPOs) — are not sortable.

Chapter 2: Tools and Platforms for Swing Trading

Like beginning some other business and calling, be it low maintenance or full time, you require a couple of significant instruments to exchange. To start with, you should open a record with a representative if you don't know now you have one. Your agent will gracefully on an online request execution stage can perform trade. It will be dependent upon you to figure out how to utilize it; however, the entirety of the steps is truly direct and straightforward to use.

Luckily, there are various intermediaries and stock trading stage alternatives accessible today that permit you to trade on the web. The financier decisions available to you will rely upon the nation you are as of now dwelling in.

On the off opportunity that you don't have a functioning trading account, it is proposed you do a Google search to discover ebb and flow surveys on dealers in your general vicinity that come suggested. Coming up next is a rundown of components you will need to consider while picking a representative:

- commissions and charges
- type of record
- platforms and instruments

Let us analyze these elements in more detail beneath.

2.1 Platforms for Swing Trading

Trading stages can shift radically from financier to business. Some business firms offer various degrees of administrations for different expenses. To do swing or position exchanges, you will need a stage that provides constant statements and a direct request process that executes promptly so you can affirm your transactions.

It would likewise be perfect to have a stage that can do ongoing graphing, give at any rate an essential degree of specialized examination (moving midpoints, and so forth.) just as provide research reports, money related information and experts' appraisals. These highlights are not completely basic; however, since you can get quite a bit of this data from destinations like Fenves and Chart Mill.

A portion of the more remarkable dealer stages will likewise have devices that do specialized examination and studies that will discover the cost and volume designs that we search for as swing or position traders. These instruments will distinguish and signal them for your thought. While these can be useful in settling on a trading choice, never indiscriminately exchange off of these instruments moving along without any more examination.

From the outset do some exploration on a site like StockBrokers.com and discover a stage that offers the accompanying:

Speculation contributions: a few agents will vary on what stocks, shared assets and Exchange-Traded Funds they will permit you to exchange. Most offer a generally decent scope of monetary instruments to trade, so once more; I figure most businesses will be reasonable.

Examination: a few steps will give elite exploration reports to supporters. A significant part of the exam you need is accessible on the web, so I don't put a lot of significant worth on this factor.

Versatile access: having portable access is "ideal to have" yet, as a swing trader, as a rule, try not to make exchanges on the fly. Mobile access to your trading stage can be a benefit now and again.

34

Training: some specialists will offer a few instructional exercises on the best way to utilize their foundation and possibly a few nuts and bolts in regards to stocks and exchanges. These are ideal to have however are not basic since the stage ought to be intended for usability, and there are numerous assets accessible to all the more likely comprehend swing trading, (for example, this book you are perusing).

Alarms: the business ought to offer alarm support that sends a book or email to a customer when a specific occasion happens. For example, on the off opportunity that you are watching a stock at a decent passage cost, you can set the alarm and afterwards rapidly act if necessary, without letting an open door cruise you by.

When considering these elements, you have to consider the components like making your profile, checking the commission and another charge alongside the sort of record you would need to begin a fruitful exchange profile.

Examining devices: you will likewise require an approach to check for purchasing openings. Luckily, you don't need a continuous scanner like Trade Ideas, which is an instrument that an informal investor would use. Some astounding checking apparatuses are accessible for nothing on the web, which I will talk about in the accompanying segment.

2.2 Tools Available Online

Luckily for the swing trader, various phenomenal free assets and online devices are promptly accessible among which a portion of the for the most part utilized and favored ones are talked about and referenced beneath:

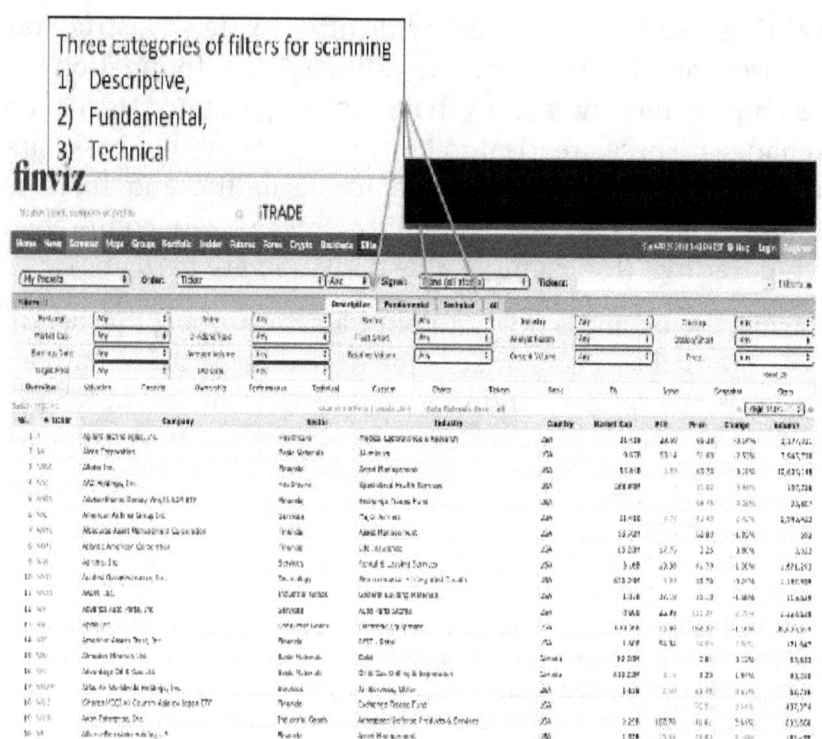

Finviz (finviz.com): the site name is short for Financial Visualizations. This site gives an enormous measure of data on the securities exchange, various segments, monetary forms, and so on. It further provides money related investigation, examination and information perception, just as astounding filtering devices. The site works admirably of summing up an enormous volume of data into outlines and guides.

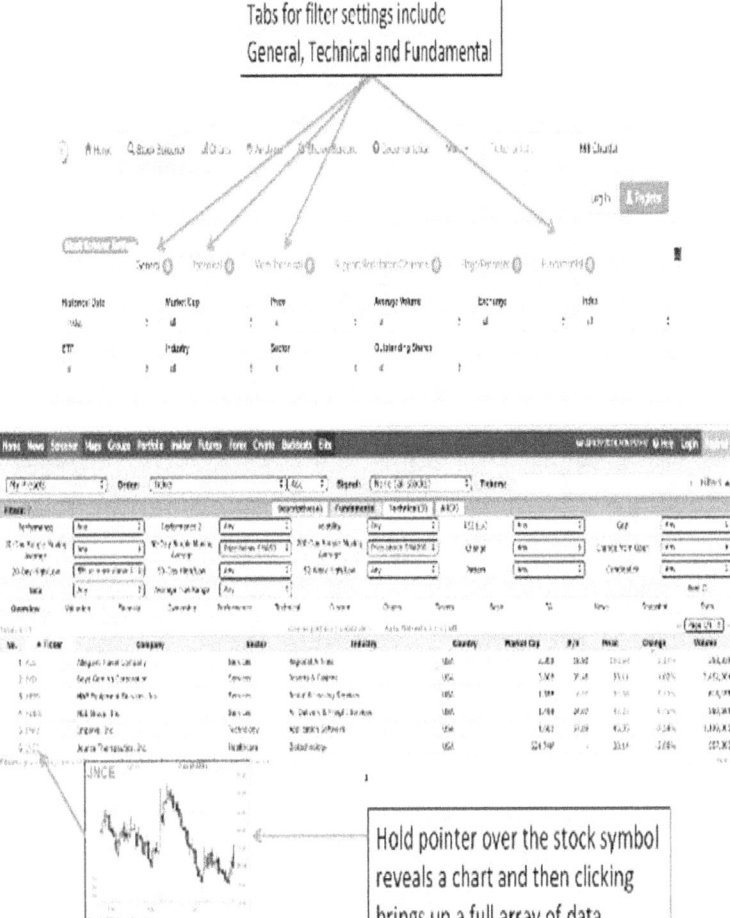

Chart Mill (chartmill.com): This site offers a significant part of a similar data given by Finviz (talked about above). The website likewise has a restrictive rating highlight that provides an evaluation on a stock's circumstance and rates the nature of the arrangement if a trader is thinking about entering a position. This is another incredible site to discover venture openings.

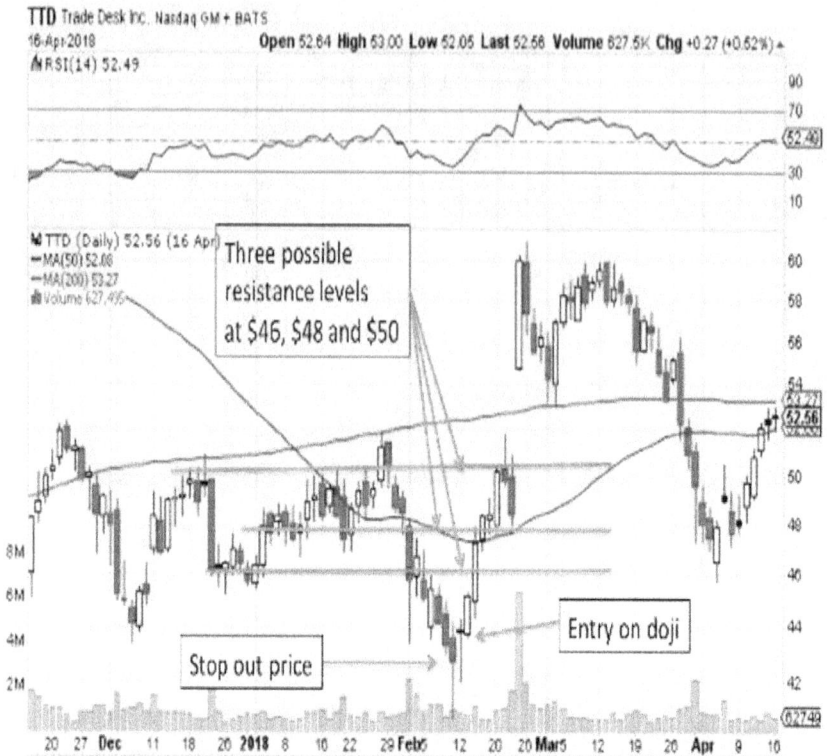

(Stockcharts.com): this is another astounding site that contains data like that offered by Finviz, including graphing devices, research information, editorial, and training. It helps discover the capacity to imagine information, for example, through the administrations offered by StockCharts.com and comparative organizations, causes us to settle on educated choices.

Estimize (estimize.com): Estimize is an open monetary evaluations stage intended to gather forward-looking budgetary assessments from free, purchase-side, and sell-side investigators, alongside those of private speculators. The site likewise has a great schedule which can be utilized to see the up and coming organization, government and industry declarations that may move singular stocks, advertise parts or the market by and large.

Stock Twits (stocktwits.com): Stock Twits is an online networking stage intended for sharing thoughts between financial specialists, brokers, and business people. Anybody can join and offer their musings and thoughts identified with various protections. There are numerous useless posts, yet the site provides an approach to perceive what is inclining and effectively trading.

CNBC (CNBC.com): CNBC is a supplier of business news and continuous market inclusion.

Hurray Finance (finance.yahoo.com): a speedy go-to site for business news, analysis and ongoing statements.

The sites recorded above are just a couple of the destinations that a swing trader can use to discover trading openings. These are principally the ones that are used and recommended to fledglings, visit everyone and become acquainted with the data, examination and checking apparatuses they offer. The checking devices that are provided for nothing on the web will probably be on a par with whatever your trader offers.

2.3 Financial Instruments for Swing Trading

There are various sorts of money related instruments that you can swing exchange with, and every last one of them has its favorable circumstances and detriments. Every broker is unique, so there might just be one specific instrument you lean toward over others depending on your hazard profile, your degree of involvement with the market, the current economic situations, your personality, and so on.

Under various instruments that you can consider for swing trading. The rundown isn't comprehensive; however, it covers the most well-known vehicles for this kind of exchange. This rundown incorporates:

- individual stocks
- Exchange-Traded Funds (ETFs)
- cryptocurrencies
- currencies
- options

Exchange Traded Funds

You can exchange ETFs available through your money market fund like how you would transfer an ordinary organization's capital, for example, Microsoft Corporation (MSFT) or Apple Inc. (AAPL). You can get them and sell them as a day exchange or hold them longer for a swing exchange. In the United States, most ETFs are set up as "open-finished" venture organizations. This sort of venture structure permits the assets to have more noteworthy adaptability in using fates and alternatives just as having the option to take an interest in security loaning programs.

ETFs have been accessible to exchange the US for around 25 years now. The Securities and Exchange Commission in 2008 of US proposed changes that released the principles on the necessities for ETFs. From that point forward, these assets have developed significantly in numbers and as indicated by the "2017 Investment Company Fact Book", ETFs currently make up about 2.5 trillion dollars in esteem.

These assets have changed altogether since the primary wide-based file finance showed up in 1993. This first store was set up to follow the S&P 500 Index. You can think about an ETF as a pool of ventures that the proprietors each own a bit of. The director of the ETF will have a lot of targets and strategies that will direct the focal point of the reserve.

Today you can discover ETFs that track everything from records and securities to stock segments, products, monetary standards, and even the instability of the market. Most as of late, a few firms have attempted to make an ETF dependent on holding a bushel of digital forms of money. ETFs can likewise be utilized to play both the long and short side of the market. There On the off chance that you speculate a segment like gold mining organizations is dropping in value, at that point you can go short on gold mining stocks by going long on DUST – an ETF that goes up in cost when the costs of capital in gold mining organizations drop.

To make things somewhat more intriguing, some ETF administrators have likewise made what is alluded to as "beta" reserves. These assets use subsidiaries like "alternatives" and "fates" to amplify the developments of the primary resource in the store. For instance, UNG is an ETF that moves with the cost of petroleum gas, which can be very unpredictable all alone. On the off chance that isn't sufficient energy for you, attempt UGAZ, which is another ETF that moves in a state of harmony with the cost of flammable gas aside from, using these subordinates, it will move 3x toward whatever path the hidden gaseous petrol resource does.

For instance, suppose the cost of gaseous petrol hops up 3% on a stock report. On the off chance that you hold the ETF UNG, the price will be up to about the equivalent 3%, however, on the off chance that you possessed UGAZ, the value of that ETF would be up 9% (3 beta occasions 3%).

Another issue with beta (additionally called utilized) ETFs is that they should be rebalanced toward the finish of each trading day. There's a considerable amount of data promptly accessible on the web. It is significant for the utilized ETF speculator to realize that their utilized holding can lose an incentive after some time, and particularly in an unpredictable non-inclining market. That implies utilized ETFs are smarter to hold in a drifting business sector (either up or down) and ought not to be held for an all-encompassing timeframe like a non-utilized ETF or general store.

- **Ride a sector:** let us envision you genuinely like the biotechnology space as a rule. There have been a few mergers and acquisitions as of late around there, and the entirety of the stocks in the area are responding decidedly. As opposed to going out and attempting to purchase up a bushel of shares in the division, you can buy an ETF like XBI, which puts resources into S&P stocks in the biotechnology area. This is a substantially more practical approach to put resources into various stocks in an area without really buying little quantities of multiple commodities.
- **Expense ratios:** ETFs have a generally low-cost balance contrasted with other speculation vehicles, for example, shared assets. You usually need to "pay to play" however, so attempt to keep these expenses as low as could reasonably be expected.
- **Portability of capital:** utilizing an ETF permits the speculator to move all through areas with a solitary exchange. Divisions regularly pivot all through kindness with financial specialists. On the off chance that you are long in one segment's ETF, and it would appear that that division is going to head lower in value, one exchange can get you out of your long position. You are presently back in real money, searching for the following chance.
- **Risk management:** utilizing a similar case of the biotechnology division being hot, how about we expect you chose to go out and purchase a couple of individual stocks in this space rather than an ETF, for example, XBI. One of them could have been PUMA Biotechnology Inc. (PBYI). While XBI has been moving higher through mid-January 2018, on January twenty-third. PBYI discovers they won't get a key medication endorsement from Europe and the stock tumbles from $94.00 at the near $65.00 twilight. In the examination,

XBI encounters a little drop of about $2.00 per share on that equivalent day. The terrible news harms XBI a piece; however, this little misfortune is nothing in contrast with what occurred with those claiming PBYI stock. Which would you reasonably possess in this circumstance? This is a basic standard of security proprietorship and features how terrible it tends to be in case you're not broadened in your portfolio. Expansion implies not having all of your investments tied up in one place, in this way, claiming an ETF spreads your hazard over the area and not in one stock. Holding singular biotechnology stocks can be especially dangerous when adverse occasions happen.

Currencies

The speculation markets can rapidly take the currency of financial specialists who accept that trading is simple. Transferring any venture showcase is exceedingly troublesome. However, achievement first accompanies training and practice. All in all, what is money trading and is it directly for you?

The money showcase, or forex (FX), is the most significant speculation advertised on the planet and keeps on developing every year. On April 2010, the forex showcase came to $4 trillion in everyday average turnover, an expansion of 20% since 2007.1

In the examination, there is just $25 billion of the day by day volume on the New York Stock Exchange (NYSE). The market might be huge, however, up to this point, the amount originated from proficient brokers, yet as cash trading stages have improved all the more retail traders have seen forex as reasonable for their venture objectives.

Forex traders take into consideration all day, every day trading money sets, making it the world's biggest and most fluid resource showcase.

While it is the biggest market on the planet, a generally modest number (~20) of cash sets are liable for most of volume and action.

Monetary standards are exchanged against each other assets (e.g., EUR/USD) and each pair is commonly cited in pips (rate in calls attention to) out to four decimal spots.

Currency costs change depending on the monetary circumstance of the nations in question, international hazard and unsteadiness, and exchange and budgetary streams, among different components.

Currency trading is a 24-hour advertisement that is just shut from Friday night to Sunday evening, yet the 24-hour trading meetings are deceiving. Three meetings incorporate the European, Asian and United States trading sessions.

Although there is some cover in the meetings, the fundamental monetary standards in each market are exchanged for the most part during those market hours. This implies certain cash sets will have more volume during specific meetings. Brokers who remain with games dependent on the dollar will locate the most size in the US trading meeting.

Money is exchanged for different estimated parcels. The miniaturized scale part is 1,000 units of cash. On the off chance that your record is supported in US dollars, a smaller scale part speaks to $1,000 of your base cash, the dollar. A lower than usual parcel is 10,000 units of your base cash, and a standard part is 100,000 units.

Individual Stocks

One of the undeniable decisions for swing trading is with individual organization stocks. Holding an individual stock can open you to a single occasion hazard. Assume you are long a stock and some negative news comes out, for example, the departure of a significant agreement, an SEC examination or a claim. This is something you might want to evade, however on the off chance that you swing exchange singular stocks, you are consistently liable to single occasion hazard.

The upside of holding an individual stock is that you can exploit a solitary stock arrangement or hot area story that is happening in some individual stocks. The cannabis segment got hot in 2017; however, there was nothing but bad ETFs in that space at that point. There were, as it may, a few clear pioneers in the business and their stock value execution was heavenly and made a lot of speculators exceptionally well off.

Select single stocks will likewise every so often perform superior to their hot segment. We should take a gander at a correlation of Micron Technology, Inc. (MU) versus the XLK Technology Select Sector SPDR Fund.

This is a case of boiling stock in a warm area that would have made for a vastly improved swing exchange

The ETF XLK expanded by about $9.00 for an addition of about 15%; however, in correlation, MU increased about $22.00 or 55% during that equivalent period. This outlines you can show signs of improvement returns by putting resources into singular stocks however you additionally take on more hazard by placing your cash into a solitary stock with the capability of single occasion chance.

Cryptocurrencies

Trading these new monetary forms has been an entirely different wilderness and has pulled in both refined and unsophisticated brokers and financial specialists. A portion of the more mainstream coins include:

- Bitcoin
- Ethereum
- Bitcoin light
- Ripple

There are a lot more digital forms of money, thus called Initial Coin Offerings (ICOs).

Swing trading these monetary forms isn't for weak-willed. These trading instruments are continually liable to single occasion dangers with declarations about hacks, misfortunes of coins, conceivable government guidelines, SEC tests into ICOs, and so forth.

They made for incredible swing exchanges when Bitcoin and others were on an explanatory run higher. In any case, similar to every illustrative race, reality set in and costs descended as quickly as they went up, leaving some excessively hopeful speculators in a ton of monetary torment. As of the composition of this book, Bitcoin and different cryptographic forms of money are unpredictable.

It is regularly known about individual brokers utilizing pointer devices, for example, moving midpoints to foresee future coin value developments. These instruments are additionally used to assess and anticipate stock value developments. Brokers are utilizing comparative degrees of 50, 100 and 200-day moving midpoints to discover zones of help and obstruction yet. It feels there is still an excessive amount of vulnerability in these business sectors to have the option to make shrewd exchanges and oversee hazard.

Now soon, there will be no considerable increases to be made in digital currencies, and trading or holding cryptographic forms of money is excessively dangerous. There are many shifted expectations and feelings on the future estimation of these trading vehicles that go from zero to "anything is possible". Until another pattern develops, swing trading these monetary forms won't be thought of.

Options

To comprehend the open doors in swing trading options you first need to see how alternatives work. The accompanying four things are required to characterize an investment opportunity

- The stock that the decision is being applied to (AAPL, IBM, and so forth.)
- Is it a "call" or a "put?"
- the strike cost
- the expiry date of the option

A "call" option allows the purchaser to purchase the underlying stock at a characterized value (the strike cost) before expiry. You would not practice that alternative except if it was productive for the broker.

For instance, FB was trading at around $170.00 in March 2018. On the off chance that you think FB will go higher throughout the following scarcely any weeks, you can purchase 100 FB shares for $17,000.00, or you can purchase a $180.00 call choice for $1.90/share that lapses April twentieth (at the hour of composing, $1.90/share was the provided advertise cost estimate to buy this $180.00 call). Your 100-share interest in FB costs you $190.00 in addition to commission ($1.90 x 100 offers). Presently you need FB to go up to over $181.90 per suggestion to equal the initial investment on the exchange ($180.00 strike cost in addition to the $1.90 you paid for the choices on 100 offers). Options go up or down in price with the hidden stock, so if you're FB shares go up to $175.00 the next day, your choice will be worth very much more than the $190.00 you paid. You would almost certainly have multiplied your cash or more with your $180.00 call rising altogether in esteem.

There is a drawback however in such a case that FB just exchanges sideways or drops value, the estimation of your alternatives will likewise drop until you get to April twentieth at which time they will terminate useless if the cost isn't over the $180.00 strike cost.

Playing a stock to the drawback is additionally similarly simple. Rather than purchasing a call, you would buy a put, which gives you a choice to sell the stock before expiry. A put purchaser benefits when the hidden stock value dips under the strike cost yet similar requirements apply to purchase puts. They can terminate uselessly, and your whole speculation will be lost if the price of the stock doesn't drop as sought after.

There likewise lies some preferred position and weakness for trading options:

Takes into account a speculator to transfer costly stocks with next to no capital.

Influence is a lot higher in choices so that little ventures can bring about large rewards; however, be cautious, they can likewise bring about huge misfortunes.

There is a period limit on alternatives, and they can terminate uselessly, and that results in a 100% misfortune.

Alternatives have period esteem in this way, as the expiry date draws nearer, the estimation of choice will drop accepting there is no development in the stock cost.

Option trading volumes are frequently much lower contrasted with stocks. This implies the spread between the offer and ask can be moderately wide, making them increasingly hard to exit beneficially.

There are additionally various systems brokers, and financial specialists utilize utilizing alternatives in blend withholding stocks. These are progressively advanced procedures and past the extent of this book. Notwithstanding, it is useful for an informed swing broker to know that these methodologies exist on the off chance that they need to accomplish more exploration and potentially utilize these procedures later on.

2.4 Assessing the Risk and the Reward

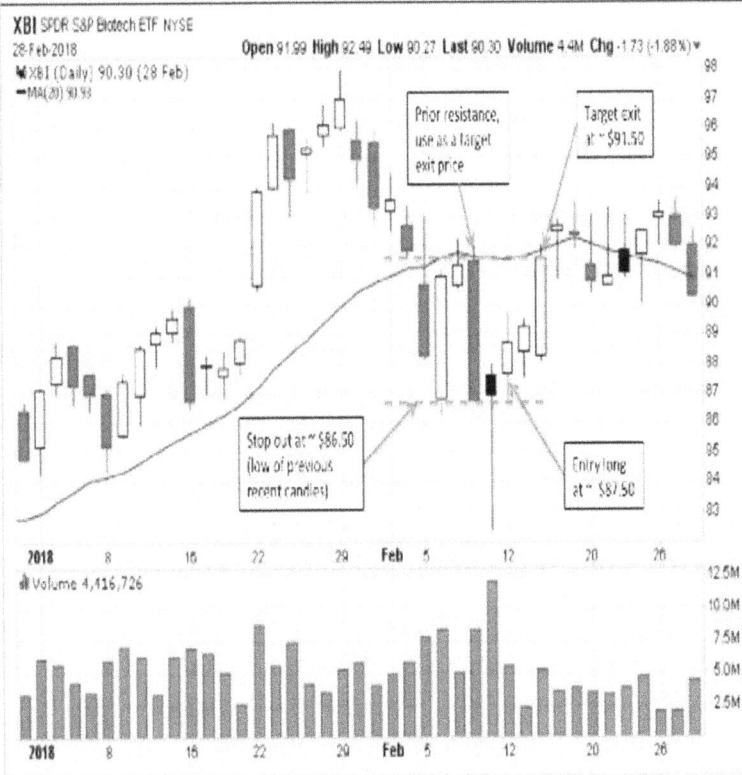

Let me move it out of the way: the win rate in trading it immaterial all alone. Numerous brokers put an abundant excess accentuation on the win rate and don't comprehend that a win rate doesn't reveal to you anything about the nature of a framework or a trader.

You can lose cash with an 80% or even with a 90%-win rate if your couple of failures are huge to such an extent that they clear out your champs. Then again, you can have a useful framework even with a win rate of the half, 40% or only 30% if you are acceptable at allowing champs to run and stopping misfortunes.

The award to chance proportion (RRR, or prize hazard proportion) is possibly the most critical measurement in exchange, and a trader who comprehends the RRR can improve his odds of getting gainful.

We should initially handle a portion of the fundamental confusions about the RRR to enable you to comprehend what the vast majority get off-base before we at that point plunge into the particulars of the RRR and how to utilize it.

Option 1: The prize hazard proportion is pointless

You regularly read that traders state the prize hazard proportion is futile, which couldn't possibly be more off-base. At the point when you utilize the RRR in blend with other trading measurements, (for example, win rate), it rapidly gets one of the most impressive trading devices.

Without realizing the prize hazard proportion of a solitary exchange, it is challenging to exchange productively, and you'll before long understand why.

Option 2: "Great" versus "terrible" reward chance proportion

How regularly have you heard somebody talk about a conventional and self-assertively picked "least" reward hazard proportion?

Indeed, even mainstream trading books regularly express that you need at any rate a RRR of 2:1 or higher – generally without knowing some other trading boundaries.

There is in no way like positive or negative prize hazard proportions. It just boils down to how you use it. You can even exchange gainfully with a prize hazard proportion of 1:1 or less.

Option 3: A terrible exchange doesn't turn out to be better with a high prize hazard proportion

Frequently, dealers feel that by utilizing a more extensive take benefit or a closer stop misfortune they can without much of an extent increment their prize hazard proportion and, accordingly, improve their trading execution. Sadly, it's not as simple as that.

Utilizing a more extensive take benefit request implies that cost won't have the option to arrive at the take benefit request as effectively and you will doubtlessly observe a decrease in your win rate. Then again, setting your stop nearer will increment untimely stop runs, and you will be kicked out of your exchanges too soon.

Beginner traders regularly legitimize "awful" exchanges where they are not trading inside their framework with a bigger reward: risk proportion. Your trading rules are there for an explanation, and a terrible transaction doesn't unexpectedly get satisfactory by haphazardly planning to accomplish a more significant reward: risk proportion.

Keeping up risk reward techniques

Secure your capital without it, you can't be a functioning swing broker.

Jettison your sense of self to submit to the market and value activity since that is all that is significant – recall, "the market can stay nonsensical longer than you can stay dissolvable".

Respect your stop-misfortune, don't let little misfortunes transform into massive disasters.

Regard your actual cost and don't take benefits too soon and subsequently change your unique exchange plan and the hazard to remunerate proportion you had built up before.

Learn and regard that having a few misfortunes is a piece of the swing trading game. Try not to think about it literally.

Continually survey your current exchanges to guarantee that nothing has changed generally in the stock, part or market. This is the main explanation you ought to consider changing your exchange plan.

Effectively deal with the size of each exchange, so you don't hazard more than about 2% of your capital.

Keep up your trading diary and survey it routinely to figure out what works and what should be changed.

Keep your brain and body fit. Perceive focuses in your life where you may be pushed or miserable and consider whether your state of mind or supposition could influence your trading choices adversely.

Chapter 3: Fundamental Technical Analysis

What is a crucial examination? In basic terms, it is an investigation of hard information on an organization, a product, a budgetary instrument, an area, and so on. That information can incorporate at least one of the accompanying:

- Earnings Per Share (EPS)
- Total Income
- Leverage: The Measure of Obligation to Value
- Price to Earning Proportion (P/E)
- Product Pipeline: Future Potential Development Driver
- Conditions That May Support or Impedimenta Specific Division/Product
- Upper Hands On an Organization May Have Over Contenders
- Company Management
- Administrative Situation and Pending Changes
- Shared Correlations
- Short Interests
- Hot Sector Manias

The critical estimates recorded above are not a total rundown, but instead, they are a portion of the more typical ones that are utilized when performing a principal investigator. The test for a large number of us is that we don't have the opportunity or the skill to, for instance, a profound plunge into budget summaries. We should leave that work and exertion to the bookkeepers and the examiners.

The critical investigation has noteworthy significance for a worthy speculator like Warren Buffett. Worth speculators usually take more prominent positions and search for moves over longer time frames because it frequently takes a year or more for different financial specialists to understand the future estimation of stock.

Some principal investigation can likewise be useful for a swing trader, and there are some exceptionally relevant factors included and discussed below.

3.1 Fundamental Analysis Factors

In any case, an essential comprehension of a portion of these critical components can be useful to a swing dealer. Specifically, you'll be better ready to perceive possibly wise venture openings in stocks. How about we grab a gander at a couple of these significant variables in more profundity and afterwards look at the one you feel is the considerable champ.

Performing a major formal investigation can take a lot of time and exertion.

Genuine top to bottom investigation of an organization's fiscal summaries requires some mastery in bookkeeping, which most swing brokers don't have.

There are a couple of principal examination apparatuses that a swing trader with next to no bookkeeping experience can utilize while scanning for trading openings:

Earnings per Share (EPS)

Profit is determined by taking total income and taking away the immediate expenses of creation. A decisive advantage is significant in the long haul for any business to keep working. In any case, the name "income" ought not to be mistaken for benefit or productivity. Benefits are determined by deducting the extra expenses of working together; for example, intrigue paid on obligation.

Total Revenue

An organization's total income is significant and can be handily seen even by speculators with restricted monetary information. This income number is a proportion of an organization's complete deals of their items or potentially benefits. It is frequently a decent marker that an organization is progressing admirably if its income is developing at a consistent pace year over year. On the off chance that the income numbers are level or dropping year over year, it shows that an organization is most likely experiencing difficulty developing its business and that benefits will probably be level or dropping too. Falling profits, for the most part, mean a falling stock cost.

Return on Equity (ROE)

The advantage for value (ROE) is a measure, communicated as a rate, of how much benefit an organization produces with the cash investors have contributed. For instance, if a financial specialist puts $100.00 into an investment account that acquires 1% every year, they expect their $100.00 to be worth $101.00 in a year. Along these lines, speculators in an organization hope to see the organization make a decent profit for their venture. The proportion of ROE shows how well the organization is getting along as far as the contributed capital.

Organizations with higher and developing ROE numbers will, in general, be all the more profoundly esteemed by speculators. Making an inquiry that incorporates organizations with higher ROE numbers is another primary hunt alternative that you can try different things with as a swing trader while doing your outputs for trading openings.

This money related proportions recorded above can be utilized to help you whenever you're searching for swing trading openings.

The degree of short intrigue gives some understanding of the slant of traders toward a stock. An elevated level of short intrigue shows that brokers are anticipating that the cost of the capital should drop substantially. Be that as it may, if some uplifting news comes out on a stock that has an elevated level of short intrigue, it can go about as a substantial impetus to drive the stock cost higher with a quick press.

A short press happens when brokers who are short a stock purchase in mass when they see the cost of that stock begin to rise drastically.

The best essential examination factor for a swing broker is finding and putting resources into hot part insanity plays.

Hot sector manias oppose most major investigation standards – sound judgment contributing is disposed of.

Probably the best open door for good returns is to discover these division insanity plays

At the point when they begin to happen, get in ahead of schedule, and afterwards, get out before the inescapable pullback or breakdown.

Debt to Equity

Most organizations need funds to begin and operate their business. They need cash to pay representatives, to buy stock, to purchase gear and PCs, and so forth. That cash can emerge out of 2 sources:

- debt and
- Equity.

The debt is borrowed cash that the organization pays enthusiasm typically on for its utilization. The bond will, likewise, should be reimbursed sooner or later. Value is cash that is put into the organization and, consequently, the financial specialist is given offers. Those offers speak to some level of possession in the organization. Eventually, the financial specialist is wanting to sell their proposals for a benefit or potentially gather profits, which are instalments that originate from the organization's interests.

Obligation and value speak to various degrees of dangers for an organization and its investors. Responsibility accompanies commitments to pay intrigue and reimburse the exceptional credit eventually. In this manner, it is a higher hazard to the organization contrasted with value, which has no such commitments. Benefit has more risk for the investors provided that the organization fails, the obligation holders typically get first pick at whatever is left of significant worth. The value financial specialists get what is left finished, and that usually is nothing.

Price to Earnings Ratio (P/E)

Price to earning proportion (P/E) is considered by numerous speculators to be the one crucial measure that beats the entirety of the others in deciding an organization's stock value development. The P/E gives you a perspective on how the market is evaluating an organization's offers comparable to its income. It is determined by taking an organization's cost for every offer (P) and partitioning by its profit per share (E). For instance, if a stock is evaluated at $100.00 per provide and it has an EPS of $10.00 per share, at that point the P/E proportion is 10 ($100.00 separated by $10.00). A higher P/E proportion implies financial specialists are eager to pay more for every dollar of yearly profit. You can utilize this number to look at how speculators are esteeming different organizations in a similar business division.

3.2 Support and Resistance Levels

Since you comprehend the candlestick option and how it shows value activity in the market for a stock, will look at how backing and obstruction levels can be utilized to anticipate future value developments in a stock. This is perhaps the most straightforward type of outlining and doesn't require any recipes or confounded estimations. All you need is your eyes and a modest quantity of innovativeness.

At the point when stocks climb, they will, in general, discover value levels that are difficult to get through. For stocks heading higher, these levels are called regions of obstruction. Then again, stocks that are dropping will, in the end, discover value levels where purchasers come in and keep the cost from moving lower. These are called regions of help. If you take a gander at an outline that contains a progression of candles over an extensive period, you ought to have the option to recognize where these regions of help and obstruction happen. You can do this for a 1-hour outline, a day by day graph or even a week after week diagram. Some of the time these

Backing and opposition levels are basic to unsurpassed casings.

Backing and obstruction line outlining is the first and most essential graphing device you ought to have the option to ace as another swing trader. When you begin doing checks, you will start recognizing potential exchange thoughts for various stocks. The following stage will be to check the value graphs of these stocks. Your eye will immediately get prepared to distinguish past zones of help and opposition, and that will assist you with surveying key-value levels for sections and exits on an exchange. A chart of NETE showing the gap up and follow through for several days, followed by a gap and fill

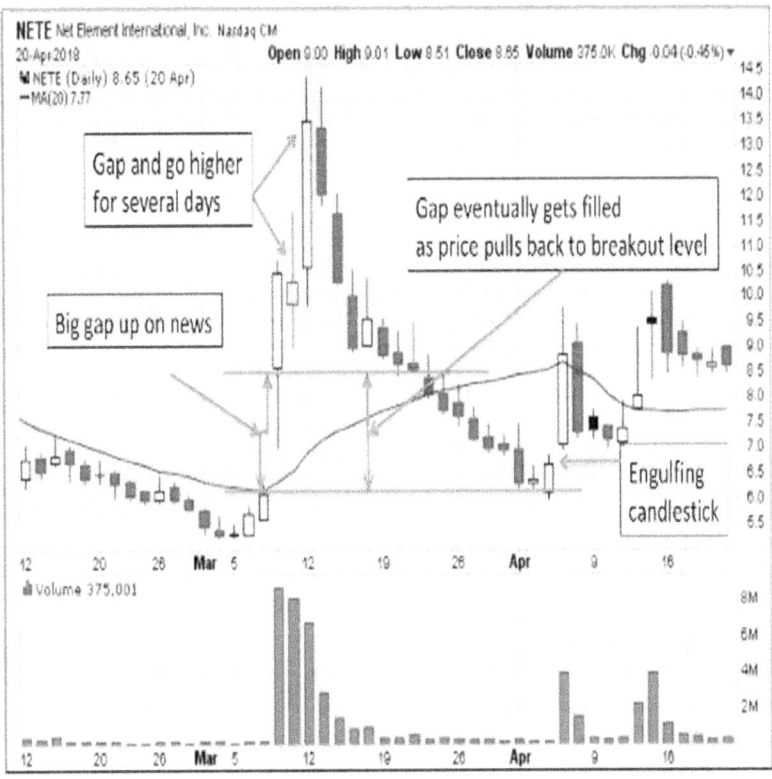

Diagonal Lines

A few dealers who work with graphs likewise search for and depend on askew trend lines. You will regularly discover these in stocks and other monetary instruments that are in long haul patterns, either up or down. These can be valuable since stocks never go straight up or down: they move in waves. These floods of value activity can gradually move a stock up or down contingent upon whether the purchasers or venders are in charge.

The test with inclining waves is that they will, in general, be progressively emotional and not entirely clear by the maker. Different pointers like moving midpoints and force markers can give comparative data, however, are not as open to a translation by the chartist. This is the reason It lean toward not to depend too vigorously on any corner to corner trend lines, anyway I am mindful that various specialized outline experts do utilize them in surveying stocks that are slanting sequentially.

Askew lines can likewise be attracted to a stock that is either drifting up or down to make a divert of trading that pattern. These corner to corner deflections of shares in a long haul upturn, or downtrend can be utilized to save you in a situation for an all-inclusive timeframe to amplify benefits. You have to perceive that if you are using slanting diverts like this; your hold time might be any longer than a run of the mill swing exchange. Your exchange could turn into a drawn-out hold, and that may not be an awful thing on the off chance that you are proceeding to construct riches.

Horizontal support

Flat help or opposition trading is necessary, however beneficial. The showcase recalls value levels, which is the reason these help or obstruction lines bode well. You may ask - for what good reason does the commercial center recollect these levels? Once more, it is an unavoidable outcome. A large portion of the learned traders and machines are taking a gander at similar diagrams and drawing the equivalent lines. They all show up at generally the same qualities for help and opposition. So usually, when one of those value levels is reached, there is extra purchasing or selling pressure contingent upon whether it is a territory of help or opposition. Minor support or obstruction regions will regularly cause value patterns to stop. Significant zones of support or obstruction will periodically make the costs in any event incidentally opposite.

The backing is a value level where purchasing is sufficiently able to hinder or switch a downtrend. At the point when a downtrend hits a help level, it ricochets. The backing is spoken to in a diagram by an even line associating at least two bottoms. The opposition is a value level where selling is sufficiently able to hinder or turn around an upswing. Obstruction is spoken to in a graph by a level line associating at least two tops

Recorded beneath are various things that you ought to know about when drawing backing or opposition lines in hourly, day by day or week by week:

i. The latter degrees of help or opposition is increasingly applicable in contrast with levels that are from further previously.
ii. Levels of help or obstruction that are tried regularly are more grounded than levels just tried once, and consequently, they are more enthusiastic to get through.
iii. Look for singular hesitation candles in the territory of help or obstruction since that is the place the purchasers and traders are battling to take control. An immersing light or Doji at support or obstruction will help affirm a potential value activity inversion.
iv. Often half-dollar ($0.50) and whole dollar numbers go about as a help or obstruction level, particularly in lower than $10.00 stocks.
v. Support or obstruction lines don't give you a precise cost. They are a higher amount of a "zone" where you will locate this level.
vi. For instance, if you attracted a line in a stock diagram and found a region of help at $21.20, you ought not to anticipate that the cost should go to and bob precisely off of that $21.20 level. Nonetheless, on the off chance that you picked your line accurately, there is a decent possibility that someplace around that level, there will be some purchasing help. The stock may skip at the $21.45

level, or it could drop to $21.00 before bobbing back. A few factors that may influence the specific bob level to incorporate by and significant economic situations on that day, the cost of the stock (does it exchange at $10.00 or $100.00 per offer) and its Average True Range (how much the stock cost fluctuates every day by and large) to give some examples.

vii. The degree of help or opposition ought to give a reasonable sign that it is in truth, a degree of support or obstruction, on the off chance that in the wake of arriving at that value the stock wallows around that value level, and doesn't obviously switch bearing, at that point it may not be regarding that level. A typical expression is "the pattern is your companion" – fumbling around a value level will, as a general rule, bring about the value activity proceeding toward the path it was going at first.

viii. If the cost of a stock gets through a degree of opposition and proceeds higher, at that point that degree of obstruction presently turns into a degree of help if a downturn in cost happens. The equivalent applies for down trending stocks that break a degree of support. That degree of assistance presently turns into an obstruction level should the stock turn and attempt to move higher.

ix. For swing trading, you can utilize different instruments to affirm backing or opposition. You can take a gander at moving midpoints like the 20, 50 and 200-day moving midpoints because a precise degree of help or resistance may likewise be going on at one of those levels

Step by step instructions to Use Support and Resistance Levels

You will regularly begin with an output of the market to recognize conceivable exchange openings.

When some possible exchanges are distinguished, you should take a gander at the graphs to check whether you can recognize levels of help and obstruction.

We should envision you have a specific stock that during a sweep has been distinguished as a possible long exchange. You take a gander at the outline and notice that the current cost is near a degree of earlier opposition. This is where it has not had the option to break higher previously. You would most likely need to pass on going long on this stock since this is a region of earlier value obstruction.

Then again, on the off opportunity that you locate a stock that is trading simply over a degree of earlier help, this may give a decent long passage from a hazard to compensate for the viewpoint. Your risk would be the value distinction from the help level to the passage cost. Next, you would hope to discover where you may anticipate that the stock cost should meet some obstruction and afterwards ascertain your hazard to reward proportion. Review that your potential prize ought to be at any rate multiple times the risk you are taking on the exchange.

Levels of help and opposition will regularly give you high reference costs for hazard and prize computations accepting you get the section cost in your exchange plan. Having a decent risk to reward proportion is significant to your prosperity as a dealer.

3.3 Moving Averages

Moving averages are one of the most regularly utilized specialized pointers over a full scope of business sectors. They have become a staple piece of many trading methodologies since they're easy to use and apply. Although moving averages have been around for quite a while, their ability to be effectively estimated, tried, and asked makes them a perfect establishment for present-day trading methodologies, which can fuse both specialized and necessary investigations.

One of the most mainstream markers to utilize is moving normal (MA). This marker takes a gander at the end value information over some undefined time frame, to determine the reasonable estimation of the advantage. For instance, utilizing a 50-day MA would take the end cost for every one of the most recent 50 days, include them up, and isolate them by 50 to get the average price. These focuses are then plotted together to make a single line, streamlining the market developments, with the goal that a trader can more readily comprehend the general pattern.

The MA is centered on recognizing or affirming a pattern, instead of foreseeing it – this is because the MA is a slacking marker, so it will consistently be marginally behind the market cost. On a fundamental level, when the price is trading solidly over the moving normal, the pattern is viewed as up, and when the cost is trading beneath the moving normal, the design is considered to be down.

A typical moving standard procedure is to search for hybrids between two exponential moving midpoints, which give a more noteworthy weighting to following value information – in contrast to a standard MA. Regularly, this technique utilizes one fast exponential moving average (EMA, for example, the 50-day EMA in the diagram beneath (the red line) and one moderate EMA, for example, the 100-day EMA underneath (the green line). The point is to search for focuses at which moving midpoints run into each other, which can flag an adjustment in the value heading. On the off chance that the quick EMA crosses the average EMA from beneath, a swing broker should seriously mull over opening an extended position. At the same time, they would go into a small area when the quick EMA crosses the moderate EMA from above.

The two fundamental kinds of moving averages are straightforward moving averages and exponential moving averages; both are midpoints of a specific measure of information over a foreordained timeframe. While basic moving midpoints aren't weighted toward a particular point in time, exponential moving averages put more noteworthy emphasis on the following news.

In this trading system, the attention is on straightforward moving midpoints; the objective is to help decide passage and leave signals, just as help and opposition levels.

How does it function?

Most trading stages plot basic moving midpoints for you; however, it's essential to see how they're determined so you can all the more likely grasp what's going on with value activity. For instance, a ten-day SMA is determined by getting the end cost in the course of the most recent ten days and isolating it by ten.

At the point when plotted on a graph, the SMA shows up as a line that roughly follows value activity — the shorter the timeframe of the SMA, the closer it will monitor value activity.

A most loved trading procedure of our own includes 4-period, 9-period, and 18-period moving averages, assisting with discovering which heading the market is drifting. The utilization of these three moving averages has been a most loved of numerous speculators and picked up a reputation in the fates showcase for stocks.

To start with, it's critical to recollect that shorter moving midpoints will embrace value activity more intently than longer ones since they're centered more on late costs. From this, you can reason that shorter moving midpoints will be the first to respond to development in value activity.

For this situation, you see basic moving midpoints traverse, which may flag a purchase or sell opportunity, just as when to leave the position (utilize straightforward moving midpoints since they give more clear signals for this situation). Note that this technique ought to be used related to the general pattern of the market.

Entry

A purchase/sell signal is given when the 4-time frame SMA traverses the 9-time frame SMA and the two of them at that point cross the 18-time structure SMA. For the most part, the more keen the push from every single moving ordinary, the more grounded the purchase/sell signal is, except if it's following a considerable move sequentially.

Thus, if value activity is meandering sideways and the 4-time frame and 8-period SMAs simply float over the 18-time frame, at that point the purchase/sell signal is powerless, in which case we watch out for cost to guarantee it stays underneath/over the 18-time frame SMA.

Though if the initial two moving midpoints shoot above/underneath the 18-time frame SMA with a reason, at that point the purchase/sell signal is more grounded. (For this situation, an affirmation of a solid upward/descending pattern can emerge out of a forceful push higher/lower from the 18-time frame SMA.)

Forceful dealers can enter the position on the off chance that they see a robust hybrid of the 4-time frame and the 9-time frame SMAs fully expecting both intersections the 18-time frame SMA. For this situation, we suggest guaranteeing that every moving is typically running toward the break and that you watch out for energy. If energy begins to wane early, it very well may be a sign of a powerless pattern.

Watch out for the general pattern by utilizing medium-term and long haul periods. If the market is inclining in either bearing, at that point, financial specialists must be attentive of retracements the other way.

Here and there value activity can backtrack forcefully, which causes the 4-time frame and 9-period SMAs to traverse the 18-time structure rapidly. Still, since it's a retracement and not part of the general pattern, value activity can come up short on steam decently fast. A design that is losing energy will become apparent sooner in the present moment SMAs.

Stop

In a perfect world, a stop ought to be set far enough away that it isn't activated rashly however close sufficient to limit misfortunes. It's fundamentally there in the event of a sharp spike off course. As a rule, the 4-time frame and 8-period SMAs will traverse the 18-time structure SMA before a stop is activated, which ought to be a sign to cut your misfortunes.

Exit

This is the place the technique turns out to be increasingly emotional. Our supported way of assault from here is to pass judgment on the quality of the pattern and continue as needs be. You can hang tight for the previously mentioned moving midpoints to recross one another or you can utilize your judgment to decide when to leave the position.

In an unbroken pattern, it's occasionally worth leaving the design when it begins to head off course over a couple of time spans because sharp pushes in either bearing can be dependent upon retracements. In powerless patterns, you will in general kindness trailing stops.

Regardless, a significant admonition sign is a point at which the 4-time frame and 9-period SMAs traverse the 18-time structure SMA, mainly if the exchange isn't working out as arranged (that is, it's a decent an ideal opportunity to get out to forestall conceivable further misfortunes).

Final points to be considered

Use stop orders for all exchanges; in any case, putting in such requests won't limit your misfortunes.

Take a gander at short and different periods; for example, take a gander at both the 10-and 15-minute diagrams at the same time.

Focus your trading system on a compelling danger reward proportion.

Watch out for the general pattern. Wary traders ought to abstain from running contrary to the natural order of things.

Have a leave technique before you enter the exchange and sit tight for the signs. Try not to let feelings cloud your judgment as the market begins to move.

Financial specialists may improve their chances of distinguishing trading by utilizing this procedure related to different examinations, which can assist with deciding the general pattern of value activity and why the market is responding to how it is. Did value activity simply break a critical opposition/bolster zone? Was there an occasion that caused value activity to spike in either bearing?

The Moving Average Crossover methodology in real life

Purchase model: USD/JPY ten-minute diagram

Notice that there is a substantial push higher in value activity after the hybrid and afterwards are a couple of chances to leave the exchange. It's additionally intriguing to take note of that when the 4-time frame and 8-period SMAs cross back under the 18-time frame SMA, it's an extremely uninteresting hybrid (value activity and the SMAs are levels), so it wouldn't lure us into getting short.

Sale example: 15-minute

NZD / USD map

There's no strong sell signal here, but the overall trend

The pair is lower, so you're comfortable getting short.

Set a stop, which is mostly discretionary, just

In case the price action suddenly goes up.

3.4 Relative Strength Index

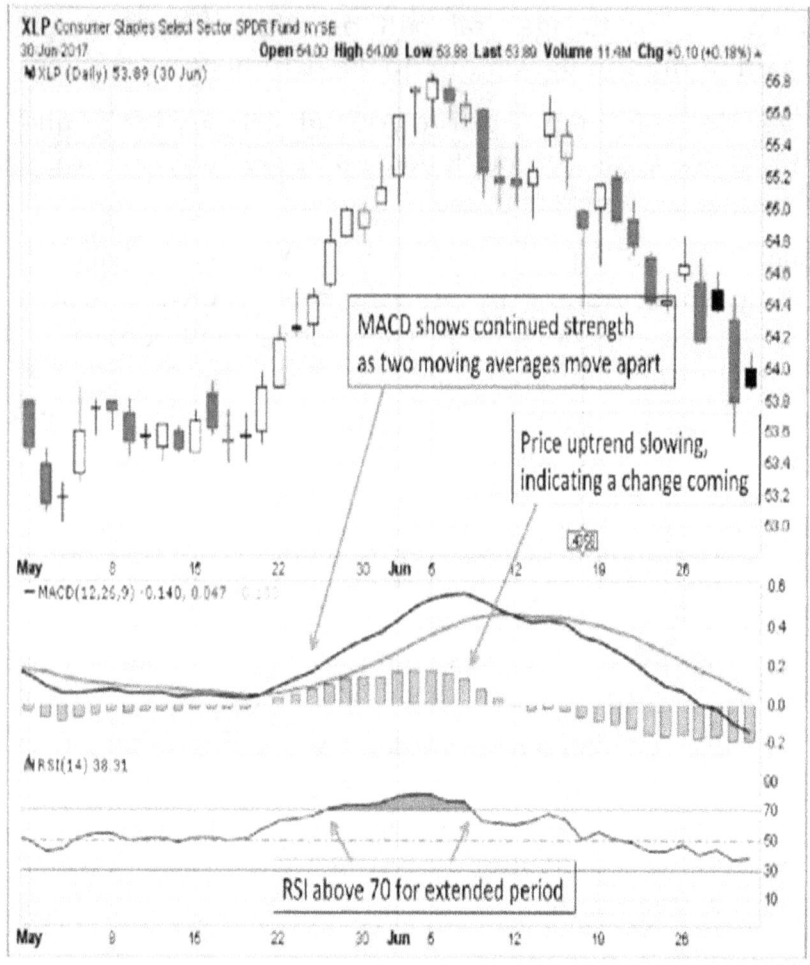

For swing trading RSI is best used to differentiate over-sold and over-bought situations. In the most part the market is deemed overbought when the RSI rises more than 70. It is generally considered oversold at the point where the RSI falls under 30. Traders use over-sold buying and selling to over-bought rates.

Shift brokers to a large degree use advanced analysis and occasionally primary review to identify trade openings.

Brokers typically use different markers for detailed inspection to help them discern the right section and quit focus.

The RSI or, in all likelihood known as the Relative Strength Index marker is one the most ordinarily utilized specific pointer with regards to swing trading.

The Relative Strength Index (RSI) is an exceptional marker that encourages monetary markets dealers to recognize when the business sectors are oversold and overbought. It is ordinarily sorted as a force pointer and assesses the market by estimating the extent of value changes.

The pointer is typically shown as an oscillator, which is a diagram line that wavers between two limits of 0 and 100.

As should be evident on the diagram over, the RSI marker is ordinarily shown underneath the trading outline as a line chart which for this situation is red. In the RSI window, you can perceive how the center zone is featured in purple. The upper level is the overbought limit, and the lower is the oversold edge. As such, every time the RSI line crosses the top border, it means that the security is turning out to be overbought. On the other side, if the RSI line crosses underneath the lower limit that is a sign the security is turning out to be oversold.

RSI Breakouts

The most widely recognized method of utilizing RSI in swing trading is to spot oversold conditions. In any case, in specific business sectors mean inversion doesn't work that well. In those business sectors, it may be smarter to utilize RSI as a proportion of pattern quality. For instance, you could attempt to purchase on a customarily overbought RSI perusing to catch another pattern.

Simply remember that pattern and breakout systems will, in general, have not many winning exchanges contrasted with mean inversion. This could make pattern swing trading more diligently to oversee mentally.

Step by step instructions to Use RSI in Swing Trading

In the two cases, the business sectors regularly will, in general, respond by a pattern inversion to address the costs. On account of an overbought condition, the business sectors costs will make a descending inversion pattern while in the oversold condition, the market costs will have an upward inversion pattern. It is this inclination of specific business sectors that are exploited in mean inversion trading.

As we have experienced over, the RSI marker is generally utilized in swing trading to distinguish when the market is about a return to its mean. As we depicted over, an RSI estimation of more than 70 is regularly considered as overbought, and an RSI estimation of under 30 is commonly considered oversold.

One conventional system that is utilized by traders is to purchase a stock when the RSI is lower than 30 and sell it when price gets higher than, for instance, 50. The limits that sign a purchase and sell signs can be changed to fit with the market and period you are playing with.

For the most part, you might want to change the limit estimates to perhaps 80 and 40 out of a growing business sector, and to 60 and 20 of every falling business sector. This is because a thriving business sector will in the general move higher before it pivots, while the inverse is valid for a dying business sector.

It is, in any case, important that during unique patterns, the business sectors may take some time before making the remedial inversion development. For example, if there is a solid bullish pattern when an overbought condition is distinguished, at that point, the market may take longer before an inversion design is started. In such cases, you may detect a dissimilarity.

An RSI dissimilarity is the point at which the RSI line moves the other way of the value chart. For instance, the RSI may have bottomed out at an oversold period, and afterwards begin to rise gradually, while the market despite everything proceeds downwards.

As such, if the RSI line pivots from a high perusing while the cost of the security despite everything makes new highs, we have a bearish difference.

Divergences could be supposed to be a more grounded sign of overbought or oversold conditions. The more extended time a dissimilarity perseveres, the more likely the market is to pivot. Realizing precisely to what extent it will take before the market pivots are hard, yet spotting divergences could be of enormous assistance when joined with different pointers or value designs.

What Are Oversold and Overbought Conditions?

To see how to utilize the RSI marker in swing trading, it is critical to comprehend what the oversold and overbought conditions are initially.

Similarly, as in any market, the standard of gracefully and request applies. Resources, including monetary resources, work on a flexible request rule. If the flexibility is more than the interest, at that point, the estimation of the benefit is destined to deteriorate. On the off chance that there is more interest than gracefully; at that point, the opinion of the advantage is well on the way to appreciate.

In money related markets like value lists, there are times when the estimation of a budgetary instrument rises excessively, regularly excessively fast. In those occasions, the cost is frequently alluded to as overbought.

Along with Other Indicators

RSI itself could function admirably in swing trading, however, combined with other trading markers or value designs; you might show signs of improvement in trading signals. There truly is nothing correct or wrong here. Trial with various tags like the ADX and MACD and check whether you can think of something that looks encouraging.

RSI is one of the most generally utilized trading markers. It works both for discovering overbought and oversold conditions, just as for characterizing breakouts that merit following.

Support and Resistance Factors

RSI can likewise be utilized as help or obstruction level. On the off chance that you take a gander at an outline and notice that there are certain RSI levels that the cost pivoted at or discovered hard to enter, you could envision value will create troubles around those levels once more.

3.5 MACD: Convergence and Divergence

The moving average union difference (MACD) marker is famous among brokers and experts, yet there's a whole other world to utilizing and understanding it than meets the eye. The MACD marker uses moving-normal lines to outline changes in value designs.

At the point when the price of an advantage, for example, a stock or money pair, is moving in one bearing and the MACD's marker line is moving in the other, that is disparity. This kind of sign should caution of a value bearing inversion, yet the flag can be misdirecting and off base.

Another kind of uniqueness is the point at which a security's value arrives at another high (or an extraordinary failure) level. However, the MACD marker doesn't. Generally, this would show that the value's heading is losing force and is preparing for an inversion. This can likewise end up being an inconsistent trading signal.

While you don't have to comprehend the math that underlies the computation of the MACD trend lines, by seeing increasingly about how the MACD pointer functions, you'll be better situated to abstain from getting tricked by its false signals or absence of signs, for example, when the cost turns, however, the MACD doesn't give any warning.

Issues with Divergence between MACD Highs (or Lows)

Brokers likewise contrast earlier highs on the MACD and current highs or earlier lows with current lows. For instance, if the value moves over a previous high, dealers will look for the MACD to likewise move over its more initial high. On the off opportunity that it doesn't, that is a dissimilarity or a common admonition sign of an inversion.

This sign is sketchy and related to the issue discussed previously. A lower MACD noteworthy cost level shows the expense didn't have a comparative speed it had last time it moved higher (it may have moved less, or it may have moved more slowly). In any case, that doesn't show a reversal.

Benefit's expense can move successive, progressively, for broad periods. If this happens after a more extreme move (more separation canvassed in less time), at that point, the MACD will show dissimilarity for a significant part of the time the cost is gradually (comparative with the earlier sharp move) rising higher.

On the off chance that a trader expects a lower MACD high method, the cost will switch, a significant open door might be missed to remain long and gather more benefit from the slow(er) walk taller.

Or then again more awful, the trader may bring a short situation into a solid upswing, with little proof to help the exchange aside from a pointer which isn't valuable in this circumstance.

The downtrend is brought about by keen descending steps, trailed by more slow descending movements. The definite value moves consistently cause a lot greater downdrafts in the MACD than more slow value moves.

It brings about dissimilarity when the following value wave isn't as sharp, however not the slightest bit demonstrates an inversion. MACD dissimilarity was available this entire day, yet the price dropped throughout the day. In the case of observing variation, a whole day of profits on the drawback would have been missed.

Another problem with regard to this sort of disparity is that it frequently is absent when a real value inversion happens. Subsequently, we have a pointer which gives numerous bogus signs (uniqueness happens, however, the cost doesn't turn around), yet additionally neglects to provide signals on various genuine value inversions (value switches when there is no disparity).

Issues with Divergence after a Sharp Move

Checking the MACD specialized pointer corresponding to value activity uncovers a couple of problems which could influence traders who depend on the MACD disparity device.

A uniqueness design between the two MACD pattern lines will quite often happen directly after a sharp value move, regardless of whether sequential. Deciding if a value moves is sharp, slow, huge or little requires taking a gander at the speed, and extent of the value moves around it.

Value energy can't always proceed so when the value starts to level off; the MACD pattern lines will separate (for instance, go up, regardless of whether the cost is as yet dropping).

After a solid value rally, the MACD disparity is not, at this point helpful. By dropping, while the value keeps on moving higher or moves sideways, the MACD is demonstrating force has eased back yet it doesn't show an inversion.

In the imagined graph, the EUR/USD is falling, yet the MACD is rising. Had a dealer accepted that the rising MACD was a positive sign, they may have left their short exchange, passing up extra benefit. Or on the other hand, they may have taken an extended transaction, even though the value activity demonstrated a massive downtrend and no indications of an inversion (no higher swing highs or higher swing lows to show a conclusion to the downtrend).

That doesn't mean uniqueness can't or won't signal the intermittent inversion. However, it must be thought about while considering other factors after a significant move.

Since uniqueness happens after pretty much every significant move, and most huge steps aren't quickly turned around directly after, on the off chance that you expect that dissimilarity, for this situation, implies a reversal is coming, you could get yourself into a ton of losing exchanges.

The Price and Trend Action Matter More

MACD difference appears to be a decent instrument for spotting inversions. It is mistaken, less than ideal data produces numerous bogus signals and neglects to flag various real inversions.

Traders are in an ideal situation concentrating on the value activity, rather than difference. For a downtrend to turn around, the cost must make a higher swing high or potentially a higher swing low.

To turn around an upswing, the cost must make a lower swing high or potentially a lower swing low. Until these happen, a value reversal is absent. Regardless of whether dissimilarity is available or not isn't significant. Brokers bring in money off value developments, not MACD developments.

MACD exclusivity - all alone - doesn't flag transposition in cost, at any rate not with the accuracy required for day trading.

This doesn't mean the pointer can't be used. Simply know about the traps, and don't use the arrow in separation. Concentrate more on value activity and designs rather than MACD uniqueness.

3.6 Technical Analysis – Patterns

Specialized examination of protections depends on the rule that previous value developments in a budgetary instrument are an indicator of things to come in the cost. Trading volume (the quantity of protections being exchanged) is frequently joined with value development to help improve these value expectation models.

The specialized investigation of stocks depends on the rule that previous value developments are an indicator of things to come moves in cost. Trading volume (the number of shares exchanged) is frequently joined with earlier value development to help improve these value forecast models.

The essentials of developing a candle and a bar diagram. Graphs containing these figures are promptly accessible on the web. There are some essential candle designs that numerous specialized brokers watch for and base their exchanges on.

Candlestick basics: how a candle or bar outline is built and what it enlightens you concerning the opening and shutting cost during a period just as the highs and lows of that period.

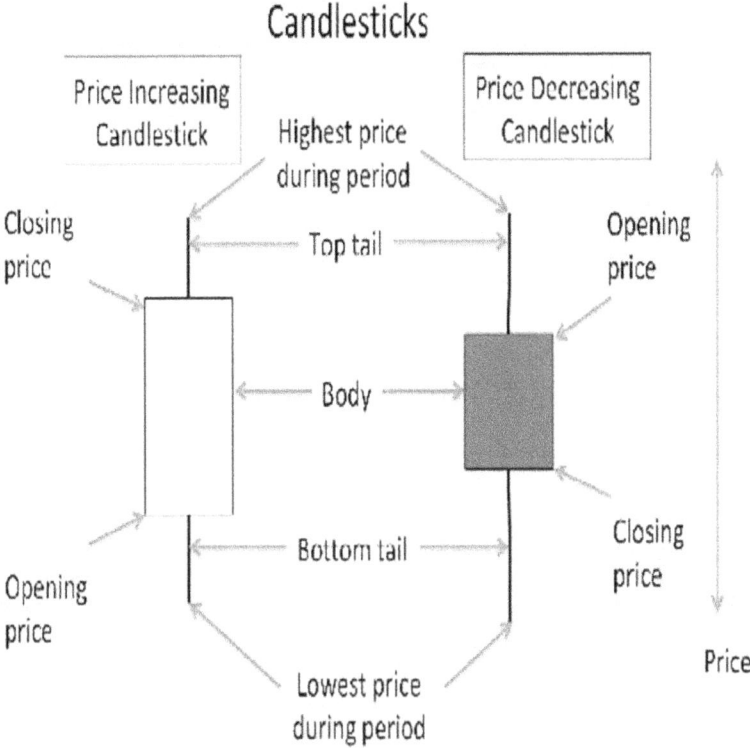

Step by step instructions to develop or distinguish a bullish candle (cost moving higher) and a bearish candle (price moving lower).

A few inversion candles were examined, including the accompanying:

Immersing flame: one huge light that is completely inundated and moves the other way of the past fire. This illustration shows examples of a gap up and a gap down between trading sessions.

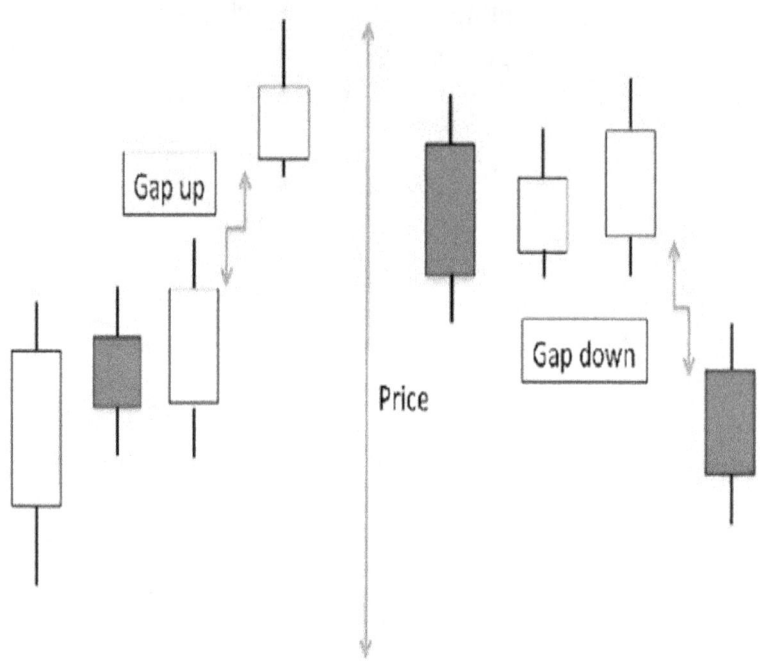

Haram cross candle: resembles a cross with a next to nobody and frequently roughly equivalent top and base tails. This chart of TZA shows an engulfing candle associated with a change in trend. In addition, the chart shows a haram cross, which also indicates a potential change in stock price direction

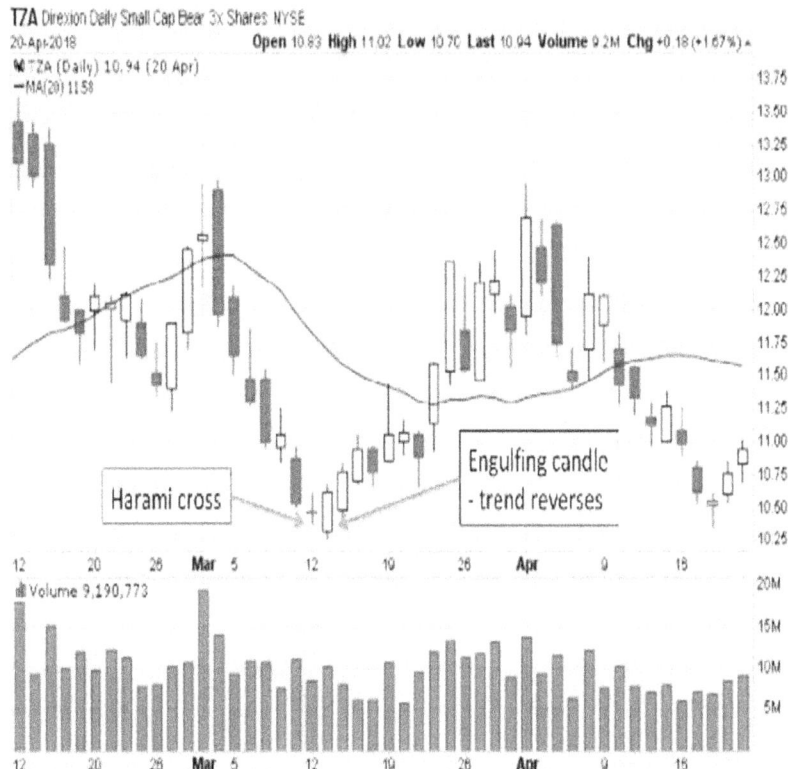

Gravestone Doji: shows that the cost of the stock opened low, it rose in price, however then dropped back and shut genuinely close to the open value, its long upper tail demonstrates conceivable bearish activity.

Dragonfly Doji: shows that the cost of the stock opened high, it dropped in price, however then expanded and shut genuinely close to the open value, and its long lower tail demonstrates conceivable bullish activity.

Inundating candles and Doji can show a pattern inversion. You can exchange these as a pattern inversion and particularly with other affirming markers like the MACD and RSI. You can likewise hope to check whether there has been some principal move that has made the stock or segment switch. This chart of PFE shows both gravestone and dragonfly Doji candlesticks with corresponding stock price reversal action

Gaps can be exchanged as a continuation exchange (the upswing or downtrend proceeds for an all-inclusive timeframe) or looked for an eruption. You can search for fixing or bottoming design because of overcompensation in value activity (which demonstrates that the purchasers or vendors are depleted and that an inversion in cost is going to occur) and afterwards take an inversion exchange. A chart of WMT shows gap in price from a close one day to the open on trading day

Gapping value activity typically happens between trading meetings. The size of the hole is frequently petite; however, on different occasions, it tends to be enormous. Bigger apertures are typically brought about by some new data that has become exposed, which influences the assessment of the brokers and financial specialists toward the stock. It could be negative news, for example, a medication test disappointment or it could be uplifting news, for example, the declaration of another item dispatch. After a hole has happened, 1 of 3 things will occur:

- gap and go
- gap and solidify
- Gap and pullback (called "filling the hole")

For a swing trader, gaps can be hard to exchange after they have just occurred. Gaps can bring about overcompensating to some news and those eruptions can be the most recent daily or they can keep going for a few days. In an improving business sector, a swing trader can take a situation during the first day of the gap up. They could take a location close to the furthest limit of the day if the stock keeps on inclining higher and finishes off the day near or at the high. There is a decent possibility under this situation (a stable market and a substantial stock value activity) that the cost will gap up again on the next day.

Another approach to playing by gaps is to utilize the gap and fill standard. Regularly the focuses where a stock gapped higher or lower become, individually, levels of opposition or backing. Eruptions in the market happen always, and in the end, these overcompensating will address themselves. A swing broker can look for top or base examples in stock that would demonstrate the purchasers or vendors are depleted and that an inversion in cost is going to occur (which will speak to a trading opportunity).

Chapter 4: Swing Trading Guiding Principles

Swing trading is a sort of trading utilizing the money related markets which endeavors to understand an increase from cost development inside a genuinely brief timeframe. This kind of trading includes typically the holding of a situation for one and a few days, making swing-trading a somewhat longer-term type of trading than day trading, in which positions are commonly shut inside a day and regularly in no time.

Swing-trading is, as its name suggests, given grasping a development in value which has just started, and swinging with the event until it is prepared to turn back. The following objective is to recognize the second before the development arrives at its defining moment and to leave the exchange right now.

To profit by this technique for exchange, it is essential to concentrate on stocks that sign patterns or examples of momentary value development. The specialized investigation is appropriate for distinguishing these chances, as the objective is primarily to pinpoint the beginning phase of noteworthy energy in value development. Essential research and inherent worth are not pertinent to the swing dealer. For a temporary increase dependent on cost development, it isn't necessary to know whether the benefit is on the direction of growth. This sort of data is applied to longer-term speculations, which fall into the classifications of position trading or purchase and hold contributing, and are regularly held for a considerable length of time or years before a benefit is figured it out.

- A useful swing-dealer will as a rule target stocks that will, in general move in rehashed or repetitive examples. By considering these examples, it is conceivable to distinguish the reasonable point in which exchange might be effectively entered and left.

- It is ideal to dodge outrageous economic situations with either bull or bear qualities, as these business sectors don't show the variances typically shown by a generally steady market.
- One tip when picking stocks with which to apply swing-trading is to concentrate on stocks with a high volume of exchanges. This dynamic trading situation gives the best probability of proceeding with energy in either an upward or descending development.
- There are programming programs accessible that help a trader to choose potential stocks to exchange, given different rules. These screening programs are available in free forms or paid updates that offer progressively customized highlights.

4.1 Defining and Building Routine Strategies

A swing trader is concerned with trying to capture the changes in value between these major lows and highs. In an upturn, a broker will be hoping to buy from these lows, or 'go deep,' and close the swing highs market. During a downtrend, traders will jump to sell from the highs to the lowest, or 'go short.'

It's hard to determine the precise high and low of each swing step accurately, but the thought is to catch; however, much of the production of value as might fairly be anticipated. Missing the particular peaks and lows is highly possible, because it may take time to say that another swing is in motion.

Two famous swing trading procedures

We've summed up two famous swing trading methods that are utilized to make a strategy for entering and leaving a market. These are:

- Breakout trading
- Trend trading

Breakout trading

Breakout trading is the methodology of accepting a situation as right on time as conceivable inside a given pattern, to exploit the market development. Swing traders will hope to recognize focuses at which the market is going to 'break out' from the range wherein it has been trading – commonly when a help or obstruction line is broken.

Breakout trading requires the broker to know how stable or powerless the market force is, which is generally determined to utilize the volume of exchanges that are occurring. This is the reason volume-weighted moving midpoints are a well-known specialized investigation instrument among swing brokers.

Trend trading

A trend transferring system depends on using specialized pointers to recognize the course of market energy. Swing trading methodologies will hope to catch a segment of this pattern, exploiting the swing high or low.

Trend traders will take a long position on the off chance that they accept the market is going to arrive at higher highs and a short post on the off chance that they figure the market will come at lower lows. They would then leave the exchange when examination demonstrated an inversion was fast approaching.

Probably the most famous specialized examination devices utilized in a pattern following techniques incorporate moving midpoints, the relative quality file (RSI) and the standard directional file (ADX).

Well known swing trading pointers

To make a swing trading system, numerous traders will utilize value outlines and specific tips to recognize expected

swings in a market, and productive passage and leave focuses. Famous swing trading tips include:
- Stochastic oscillator
- Relative strength index

Stochastic oscillator

Like the RSI, the stochastic oscillator is an energy pointer. It thinks about the latest shutting cost to the past trading range for a given period – generally 14 days. The hypothesis behind the stochastic is that it showcases energy changes in front of market volume or the value itself, making it the primary marker. In this way, by trading dependent on energy, a trader can endeavor to anticipate the swings.

The stochastic is introduced as two lines – the pointer line (the dark line on the underneath graph) and the signing line (the red speckled line beneath). These lines waver on a scale between zeros to 100. On the off chance that there is a perusing 80, the market would be considered overbought, while a perusing under 20 would be regarded as oversold conditions.

If the two lines cross, it is regularly a sign that an adjustment in advertising bearing is drawing nearer. On the off chance that the pointer line ascends over the signature line, swing dealers should seriously mull over opening a long position – except if the qualities are over 80. What's more, if the pointer line falls lower than the signature line, swing brokers should think about opening a short position – except if the qualities are under 20.

Relative strength index (RSI)

When a pattern is recognized, a broker could consider utilizing a force pointer to attempt to catch swings in the general trend. A well-known force marker is the RSI, which swings brokers can use to decide whether a market is overbought or oversold – which means the market could be arriving at a 'swing'.

In an upswing, a move out of the oversold region as shown by the RSI may be a sign to purchase an exchange. An overbought sign might be a sign to leave the trade. In a downtrend, a move out of an overbought region may be a sign to enter a short exchange, while an oversold sign might be a sign to leave the brief exchange and not exchange against the pattern.

Step by step instructions to begin swing trading

There are two different ways to begin swing trading, contingent upon your degree of certainty and mastery.

Swing trading is a trading style that centers on attempting to catch a part of a more significant move

It depends on the suspicion that market costs once in a while move in an orderly fashion, and that traders can discover opportunity in the minor motions

Swing trading works by recognizing gainful occasions to enter exchanges dependent on two unique sorts of swing: 'swing lows' and 'swing highs.'

You may not generally pinpoint the specific high and low of each swing move, yet the thought is to catch however much of the value development as could reasonably be expected

Swing traders can hold their situations for time spans extending from a couple of moments to longer than a day, as the length of a swing exchange relies upon the time period of the pattern

Two famous swing trading methodologies are extended trading and breakout trading, the two of which see momentary market developments

Swing traders will utilize specialized examination devices like the RSI and the stochastic oscillator

4.2 Option trading advanced technique for Swing Trading

An option is a subsidiary money related instrument that gives the holder or purchaser the privilege; however, not the commitment to accomplish something as an end-result of an instalment or premium. In budgetary markets, alternatives additionally have a strike or exercise value that decides at what level the holder can purchase or sell the hidden money related resource. Options additionally have a termination date past which the alternative stops to exist.

Alternative brokers utilize an assortment of options methodologies that include purchasing as well as offering at least one option to take either directional or showcase impartial perspectives on the fundamental resource advertise.

They additionally usually use charts called option payout or result profiles to get a visual feeling of what the option system will pay off on its termination date for a scope of essential market esteems, for example, the one demonstrated as follows.

Luckily, for a directional trading system like swing trading, you can undoubtedly figure out how to trade alternatives to execute your market see. The means beneath disclose how to utilize a straightforward alternative methodology, such as purchasing a call or put, to swing exchange any money related resource showcase where options are promptly accessible.

Stage 1: Select an Asset

The initial phase in swing trading utilizing options is to pick a fundamental resource for an exchange where you have distinguished a trading opportunity. Swing traders will frequently screen a few resource markets to have a unique possibility of finding a decent arrangement for an exchange.

While choosing an advantage, search for a benefit showcase due for a remedy as controlled by an energy pointer, for example, the RSI, for instance. This specific pointer is a limited oscillator that proposes that a market is overbought when its worth is over 70 or oversold when its value is under 30.

Hope to sell a market at RSI values more than 70 and get it at costs under 30. If you need much increasingly solid swing trading signals from the RSI, you can hold up until you see something many refer to as cost RSI disparity happening, which implies the cost makes a further extraordinary in a move, for example, hitting another high. However, the RSI neglects to do that. That is a shockingly better swing trading signal that the market is expected for an unavoidable adjustment.

Stage 2: Choose a Direction

When you've distinguished a market and utilized your favored type of market examination, regardless of whether specialized as well as crucial, to discover a trading opportunity with a decent hazard/reward proportion of at least 2 to 1, for instance, at that point you may feel great taking a directional market see on the fundamental resource utilizing call and additionally put alternatives.

For instance, on the off opportunity that you think the market is going to rise, you would utilize a call option to go long the hidden market you wish to exchange with restricted drawback chance and boundless upside potential.

On the other hand, on the off opportunity that your view was that the market was going to fall, at that point you would instead purchase a put alternative to go short the fundamental resource, again with constrained drawback hazard and boundless upside potential.

The option result profiles underneath appeared at lapse for long call and put positions shows how your misfortunes are restricted to the premium paid if your directional view ends up being wrong. Likewise, possible benefits on an option position are boundless and begin to collect past the breakeven point where the additions on the post surpass the premium paid.

Stage 3: Pick a Strike Price

The strike cost of an option decides its cost. All in all, the more alluring the strike cost of an option is comparative with the overall market cost for the hidden resource, the more that alternative will cost. Additionally, the more extended a replacement of a specific strike cost has until lapse, the more costly it will be.

At the point when strike costs are superior to the overall market, they are supposed to be "in cash" or ITM. An option with an ITM strike cost likewise has "inborn worth," which is equivalent to the distinction between the overall market cost (for the alternative's conveyance date) and the strike cost.

At the point when an alternative's strike cost is directly at the prevailing market, it is "at the cash" or ATM, and when at a level more awful than the predominant market, it is "out of the cash," or OTM. Both ATM and OTM alternatives have no inherent worth.

Most swing dealers are hoping to benefit from generally momentary directional moves in a market, so they will presumably pick a to some degree OTM option that they expect will go ITM decently fast so they can sell it back.

This is because options have time and incentive just as intrinsic worth and time esteem rots progressively rapidly as time advances toward lapse. This urges a swing trader to need to sell back any option they purchase at the main open door when a decent benefit introduces itself.

Stage 4: Decide on an Expiration Date

Picking a lapse date will, to some extent, reflect what extent you figure it will take for the fundamental market to arrive at your target. You will, for the most part, need to pick a shorter-term option if you figure the move will be quick or a more extended term alternative on the off chance that you think it will take some time.

Mostly, as a swing dealer, you would prefer not to pick an alternative that lapses too early since it may wind up being useless at termination. Then again, you might not have any desire to purchase an option with a termination date excessively far later on account of the relative significant expense.

Many swing dealers will pick around multi-month alternatives or options on the close to prospects contract, as long as it is over a multi-month away, since that will, as a rule, give them enough of an ideal opportunity for their view to work out before termination.

Stage 5: Plan Your Entry

Exchange passage timing is regularly done utilizing specialized examination. Since swing brokers exchange both with patterns and with adjustments to those patterns, they first need to distinguish the typical pattern, assuming any, in the advantage they are taking a gander at.

When trading with the pattern, swing brokers will search for a remedial pullback to set up a situation toward the model. When the withdrawal is by all accounts losing energy, as motioned by an RSI level in the overbought or oversold domain in a perfect world indicating disparity concerning the value, they will detect everything looks good to step into the market.

Stage 6: Execute Your Trade

When an opportunity to exchange has shown up, it's an ideal opportunity to execute as per your trading plan. For instance, you could purchase a to some degree OTM call option if the general pattern is higher or an OTM put option if the market is drifting descending.

It's additionally imperative to recall that how you exchange is similarly as significant as where you trade, so ensure you pick the correct specialist as your trading accomplice. Exchange costs, including managing spreads and charges, can indeed include after some time on the off chance that you exchange much of the time as a swing trader.

Stage 7: Manage the Position

When you've executed an exchange and have a position, you risk misfortune, even though since you bought an option, your hazard will be constrained to the top-notch you paid for it. You will likewise need to watch the primary market and deal with the option exchange fittingly.

On the off chance that you buy an OTM alternative, you can expect to sell it when the fundamental market arrives at the strike cost with the goal that it becomes an ATM. This will likewise bring about the option of getting additional premium as its time esteem increments.

Contending with potential additions will be the time rot that happens for each entire day an alternative draw nearer to its lapse date. This implies you'll need to sell back the alternative situation at the most punctual accessible chance to abstain from having an exchange dependent on a directionally stable view lose cash because of unreasonable time rot.

On the off chance that the market despite everything appears as though your exchange will work out in the long run, yet the transient move you were planning to profit by neglected to emerge, you should seriously mull over giving it more opportunity to happen as intended.

You can do this by executing a schedule spread or turn out an exchange that includes selling back the near term alternative you own and buy a more drawn out term option of a similar strike cost. This keeps you from taking misfortunes because of the actively expanding time rot on close to the cash options as their termination draws near.

At that point, locate a trustworthy intermediary so you can begin executing your new swing trading procedure.

Here's a simple beginning stage to recall – purchase calls if you think the underlying stock is going up and puts on the off chance that you believe the underlying stock is going down.

You'll have to distinguish a pattern in a specific stock only like trading ordinary offers. Utilizing specialized examination can pinpoint trends and help recognize great spots to execute exchanges.

On the off chance that you think stock in a downtrend will keep on descending, purchase puts. If you figure the descending pattern will turn around, buy calls. When you've built up whether you need calls or puts, you can proceed onward to picking a strike cost and lapse date.

Picking Expiration and Strike Price

A precarious aspect regarding executing alternatives exchanges is you have to figure the correct bearing, yet the stock needs to move that route inside a specific period. When purchasing options, you'll have to settle on a strike cost and lapse date.

Strike Price – The cost at which the purchaser of the alternative has the privilege to buy the underlying security.

Note that the option purchaser doesn't need to execute at the strike cost – that is the reason they're called options. Options get progressively costly the closer the strike cost gets to the real value of the primary resource. If a strike cost is reached, the alternative is supposed to be 'in cash'.

Termination – Options trading is troublesome because of the time estimation of the agreement joining with the natural opinion of the fundamental security. Being correct and being on time qualifies you for more prominent compensations with options. However, you have to pick the best possible lapse for your trading methodology. All alternatives lose an incentive as they approach lapse and will terminate uselessly.

Conclusion

The objective of swing trading is to recognize a general pattern and catch more significant increases inside it. Swing brokers mean to accomplish gains with their trading account that will be bigger than what they could have earned with day trading.

Clear dangers and commission costs are extraordinary and can be higher with swing trading than customary venture strategies. So swing brokers must observe these to keep them from getting a lot into any benefits they may accomplish. Moreover, because swing trading is progressively powerless to advertise unpredictability, the danger of enormous misfortunes relating to your past are some of the underlying ventures are greater.

If you are new to trading, it is recommended that you begin rehearsing the procedure first to check whether it will work for you and your circumstance. You needn't bother with an investment fund to practice, and everything that you require to begin swing trading is accessible for nothing on the Internet. As another dealer, you can do what is designated "paper trading", where you experience the way toward filtering for exchanges, distinguish openings and profess to enter the transaction. Start with a non-existent record size that is equivalent to what you mean in the first place on the off.

Swing trading is a sort of trading utilizing the money related markets which endeavors to understand an increase from cost development inside a genuinely brief timeframe. This kind of trading includes typically the holding of a situation for one and a few days, making swing-trading a somewhat longer-term type of trading than day trading, in which positions are commonly shut inside a day and regularly in no time.

Swing-trading is, as its name suggests, given grasping a development in value which has just started, and swinging with the event until it is prepared to turn back. Recognizing a value development which has initiated to swing in either an upward or descending bearing as a piece of fruitful swinging exchanges. This start of a swing is an ideal opportunity to enter the trade.

www.ingramcontent.com/pod-product-compliance
Lightning Source LLC
Chambersburg PA
CBHW050244220526
45465CB00002B/549